THROUGH THE  OW

JIM TERBUSH

*"Peter's story is a touching journey into
the true meaning of Servant Leadership"*

-CHRISTIE HICKS, Director of the Peter Terbush
Memorial Outdoor Leadership Summit

THROUGH
THE
VALLEY
OF THE
SHADOW

Jim Terbush

.

ISBN: 1502583127
ISBN-13: 9781502583123

Cover art: Yosemite Valley with Half Dome in the background.

"The story of Peter Terbush's too-brief life is inspiring and moving. The message is clear: no matter how many years you're given, you can strive toward greatness by living with an adventurer's spirit and a servant's heart."

– Keith Wall, coauthor of *Encountering Heaven and the Afterlife* and *Real Life, Real Miracles*

Table of Contents

THROUGH THE VALLEY OF THE SHADOW

Even though I walk Through the Valley of the Shadow of Death, I will fear no evil, for You are with me.

Prologue

Some people prefer to read novels but I've always enjoyed biographies. It seems to me that enough things happen in real life that are amazing, and stir the imagination sufficiently to inspire. My son Pete and I read the classic accounts of famous adventurers together; Shackleton, Shipton, Tilman, Herzog, Slocum, Cherry-Garrard, Lindbergh and Mawson. Some were written shortly after the particular events occurred, many of them were written years later. The ones that we particularly enjoyed showed incredible personal courage through epic hardship, "close calls" and frequently "one man against the elements". I think Peter learned a tremendous amount from these books and they had a way of inspiring him to try new things, think big thoughts and they prepared his mind for action. I can imagine him thinking to himself "I can do that". It was an unusual education but then Pete was an unusual guy. If this book inspires others to be a little more prepared, adventurous and resilient, especially during severe hardship, then Peter may have contributed to that collective experience.

Second, I have in the back of my mind the young people who meet annually in Gunnison Colorado where Peter went to school. This rendezvous, The Peter Terbush Outdoor Leadership Summit, at Western State Colorado University, has a special meaning for me as the story of Peter continues to unfold through the lives of others. I look forward to being with them each year and to share some of these stories. This book is specifically written for the Summit students as they learn to be "servant leaders and mountain guides" in the high Rocky Mountains. I hope they get a taste of what it was like to be Peter from this short book.

This is also a love story; about a father's love for his son; about discovery, growing up together, love of the outdoors and adventure and a love of God our creator. Pete soaked in these things like a sponge. I also believe he was given help as he walked through dangerous circumstances and dangerous places, similar to the 23rd Psalm, and did not fear evil. His courage was based on more than his own strength. As I grow older I realize that we are surrounded by heroes; people like my father and mother, people of awesome character, of courage, self-sacrificing people whose life experiences have made them wiser, more caring, and better able to anticipate the future. I have had the good fortune to meet a number of these people, be mentored by a few and learn a couple of life-lessons along the way. I tried to pass these good things along to my son.

This book could have been written years ago but now, a decade or so after the events, I feel compelled to do so, before the memory of the events fade and the persons who were actually involved move on. I had always thought that writing a book about Pete would be difficult, but perhaps not for the reasons you imagine. Like most non-authors, I was too busy to write a book and could not fit it in to the schedule. Fortunately, almost by accident, I was given some time to reflect and accomplish the task. I also believed it would be too difficult to resurrect a lot of old memories. However, it turned out to be a gift and a real healing experience. Finally, I had friends who actually knew something about writing a short book and they were invaluable in continuing to send encouragement my way. I only hope that you can enjoy these musings and perhaps find inspiration and joy through the life of one who lived well.

I want to particularly thank to following people who helped me; fact check, improve my writing and encouraged me to keep at it; Carol Leff, Jim Jackson, Keith Wall, Paul Harris and Jim Davidson.

Jim Terbush
Manitou Springs Colorado

PART ONE

A LIFE WELL LIVED

10 PM in rural Colorado, in a snowstorm and a long way from a hospital.

Leigh's maternal instincts were spot on, she said "take him, take him!" and acted like she was going to get up out of bed. I wrapped him in a towel (with the placenta still attached) and set him in the bathroom sink to go back and check on my wife. She was my number one priority. Leigh was already up and feeling much better. She was rushing around the room to get dressed. Since we were ready for bed before this happened, I pulled on some old coveralls grabbed my boots and yelled for her sister Kippi, to come upstairs. "I just had the baby", Leigh said, "but what do we do now and where are we going to take him?" There was another miracle in the works. In the months before Denver based Swedish Hospital had built a minor emergency center just to the north of Castle Rock. It had opened just the month before in December with much celebration, and was staffed by nurse practitioners. It was the only facility for 35 miles in either direction. We decided to head there and get some help.

Things take on somewhat of a blur at that point. I remember Kippi driving the Scout out into the snow and I was in the front passenger seat, holding the baby, still wrapped in the towel with the placenta on top of him and doing mouth-to-mouth resuscitation on this little guy. Actually my mouth covered his entire face and I could not tell if he was breathing any on his own. The unbroken powdery snow came up to the front bumper, pushed away to the sides and we were off for the minor emergency center. It was about 3 miles away and Kippi seemed fearless. At one point we ran off the road going around a sharp corner. As we slid sideways, Kippi was praying out loud, "Oh Jesus!, oh Jesus!, oh Jesus!", and pumping on the brakes. Without stopping, she then hit the gas, the big tires dug in and we bumped back up onto the road. We made it to the minor emergency center, the lights were on, people were in there and we rushed inside the building.

We must've been quite a sight as the staff came out into the lobby to see what was going on. I was shouting for oxygen and an incubator and I don't remember what else. We looked wild, yelling, holding something in the towel and coming in out of the dark and snow. I was still in my coveralls and had never bothered to put on the boots. "Who are you and what is this?" was the cool response from one of the staff. Pretty quickly however they sorted out the situation and began to assess our son's condition. They just "happened to have" an incubator, which had been donated when the center opened, and placed him in it. He was very premature, 14 weeks early and with a precipitous birth at home, his chances were not good. But God had a different plan in mind, and another miracle. On call that night, just up the hill in his big adobe house was Dr. Frank Martorano. Frank is a pediatric intensive care physician and he cross-country skied down to the minor emergency center when he got the call. He was able to do things for newborns that probably only one doctor in 1000 could have done. Frank came in and was instantly in charge. He asked a few questions and then went about his duties making sure that the basics were accomplished. When he found out I was a medical student he also began teaching, as he was resuscitating our son. "Well you got him here warm, that's a very good thing". Frank inserted an oxygen cannula to a small Dixie cup and placed it next to the infant's nose and mouth. He then inserted an IV into the saphenous vein on his leg, not easy in an infant of any size. "He will need a little glucose and fluids to keep him going". Finally Frank took some aluminum foil and wrapped him up to help maintain his temperature. He looked like a little baked potato.

The weather was too bad for the Flight for Life helicopter to come down from Denver. Instead Children's Hospital sent a pediatric ICU staffed ambulance behind a snowplow. Frank turned to me and said "Jim what about your wife?" She had stayed at home by herself when we rushed out the door. Frank gave me some medication to help her uterus contract and antibiotics to prevent her from getting an infection and Kippi and I went home to be with Leigh while we waited for the ambulance. Ever resilient, Leigh had already cleaned up the bedroom and taken a shower before we got back. Giving birth at home (unexpectedly) is a dangerous business. We knew the situation was bad but at the time we did not know the statistics. In 1978, 88% of babies born at 26 weeks died. Home births had worse numbers. Of the 12% that survived the majority were significantly disabled. This was when back when babies could be blinded by too much oxygen and the greatest danger was stiff lungs due to lack of maturity, (specifically lack of surfactant).

Together we sat down on the bed and prayed, for the life of the baby and for strength to believe that God was still in charge. We did not know if this was going to be the little boy we had hoped for. I got back in the Scout and followed the ambulance and snowplow back up I-25, to Children's Hospital in Denver. I stayed in one of the on-call rooms that I had previously used during a pediatric rotation there but did not sleep as they worked on my son. So many couples are faced with the situation of a pre-mature birth, it could almost be described as an epidemic. During the night my wife and I, separated by many miles, prayed together that this would be the little boy we had hoped for and that God would heal him. In that span of hours, independently, without any phone calls to each other, we both believed and we bonded with our son. We trusted God and accepted that this was his plan for us. We had already picked out a name, he was going to be Peter James Terbush.

Pete was in the hospital three months, and it seemed like he had almost every complication that severely premature infants could have. He weighed 860 gm at birth but dropped to 720 gm after about a week. We moved him to the University of Colorado where I was attending medical school because our medical insurance couldn't keep up with the mounting expenses. At the teaching hospital we qualified for indigent status and the hospital wrote off almost all the bills. In 1978 neonatal intensive care had come a long way but not nearly to where we are today. Pete had apnea episodes where he would stop breathing, we were told about hemorrhage into the brain, he required transfusion five times and we were warned about an infection in the bowels called necrotizing enterocolitis. He had monitors, tubes and wires everywhere. He looked like a ghastly lab experiment. Initially we could not even pick him up and hold him. We watched as other babies left the neonatal intensive care unit (NICU), some went home and some did not. There were lots of other anguished young couples. There were even babies smaller than ours, but not by much. The NICU staff members were tremendous. One Bobbi Stewart RN "extraordinaire", in particular. She cared for Pete (and his parents!) the entire time he was in the NICU. She essentially adopted him as her own baby. As the young Pediatric Residents and Interns came by each day for rounds they explained to us the nature of his latest worrisome diagnoses in detail and the possible consequences. We took those problems home and wrote them on a prayer list. When we were able to believe that God could heal our son from each specific condition we crossed it off the list. When we were told that Peter had survived the night and recovered from each problem we wrote down the date. That list, written on the back of an envelope, remained taped to our refrigerator for several months. It remains in his baby book as a record of God's faithfulness.

At the low point we were really quite desperate and needed some Hope. I believe that God helped me then in a supernatural way when I was praying. It was a voice inside my head but very clear. **"I have a plan and a purpose for Peter that you do not understand**

right now". It is really the only time in my life when I can remember hearing, very distinctly, God saying anything to me. I held on to that promise over the years. It particularly sustained me through Pete's time in the hospital. Most young marriages are at risk when there is loss of a child or birth of a severely premature infant. Thankfully we were surrounded by loved ones. The little community of Castle Rock published an article in the local paper about the miracle baby; there were praying grandmothers and grandfathers, friends, family, church members and residents of our local nursing home who all became involved in the prayers for Pete. Eventually he began to gain weight.

Pete left the hospital at three months of age and 4 pounds.

Chapter 2
Adventuring Around the Planet

Soon after Peter came home we moved to California. I was in the Navy and we were assigned to Camp Pendleton near San Diego for my internship. Internship was a tough year but especially for my wife. Pete was sick with frequent ear infections, he would not eat well and seemed to sleep all the time. Leigh was a young wife and mother, alone with two small children most all of the days and many of the nights, far away from her family. I was busy learning my profession and received positive feedback but when I arrived home I was exhausted and provided little support. At one point during the year I was called into my boss' office (Dr. Robert Higgins RADM MC USN ret.) and told that all interns were going to be required to serve at least one year in an operational assignment. I complained that this was not what I had signed up for and would be a real break in my education. Then he said "go on, get out of here, it'll be good for you". I was just sure that a year away from training before completing my residency in family practice would be devastating to my future career as a physician. Instead it was a life saving gift for my family. Thanks Sir!

We were then assigned to Pensacola Florida for flight surgeons' training. This turned out to be the very best possible course for us. Pete got pressure equalization tubes in his ears to help prevent infection and developmentally he leaped ahead. Leigh and I got to know each other again in the warm relaxed environment of Northwest Florida. We had time to go boating, SCUBA diving and fishing and take long walks on the sugar white sand beaches. Meanwhile I was learning to fly and how to take care of pilots and what to do in a survival situation. It was terrific. But when the time came to learn of our onward assignments as a new flight surgeons I was puzzled. I had asked for an assignment in Europe accompanied by my family, (talk about being optimistic). My friends had mostly learned of their assignments already, but no one had called to tell me. When I went in to work the next day I saw my name on the list, we were going to Keflavík Iceland for two years. Be careful what you ask for.

Keflavik Iceland was a NATO base where the US and other military forces guarded the approaches to the North Atlantic from the Soviets. There were a variety of aircraft assigned to the base and for a new flight surgeon it was one of the most exciting jobs possible. In addition I had duties at the small hospital and frequently I was the only doctor in the emergency room. Peter and big sister Julia would be bundled up in snow suits to go out and play in the wind and sleet. Moms would form a human chain to pass kids hand-to-hand to get them on the school bus. A great fear talked about at elementary school was being knocked down by the wind and "blown away". Giant dumpsters would start moving on the ice and be found in the morning many yards away from where they started. In certain weather conditions everyone was restricted to staying indoors, wherever they were located. I remember walking to the hospital on occasion with ice axe, goggles and crampons just to go the 100 yards or so from our housing. I loved it.

Because it was a small base and isolated, the young families got to know each other very well. We shared kids, meals, holidays and when the guys were deployed the gals got together. One of the great benefits of this job was the opportunity to take the family on rest and recuperation (R&R) flights to Europe. Over the course of two years we managed to go to; England, the Netherlands, France, Germany, and Portugal. We brought a new four-wheel-drive with us, another Scout, and took it all over the island. We never let the weather be an excuse for not heading off the base. Groups of us would circle the four-wheel drives into a wind block and we would picnic. We took the kids hiking and visited the hot springs. Natural geo-thermal hot water was stored in giant tanks above the town and then pumped through homes and businesses and finally through large greenhouses where tropical fruits and vegetables were raised under glass. When the hot water had completed its journey it ran down through a pipe and exited a few hundred yards from the ocean. This water, still clean and hot (about 104°), ran down a rocky ditch with many small pools along the way. Our family would run across the snow with parkas over swimsuits in jump into the delicious hot water. Peter, then three, and just a little guy, climbed his first mountain in Iceland. It was not much more than a small volcanic bump a few hundred feet high but he seemed pretty excited. This was also when we met our friend Dr. Tony Jones in northern Wales. He was a colorful character, born in South Africa and served with the Royal Air Force. He was the one who first put the kids on a rope and allowed Pete and Julia to climb up some easy rocks.

After Iceland it was time to complete my medical training and we headed back to the states to Bremerton (Seattle area) Washington for two years. We all loved the Pacific Northwest and we tried to take advantage of every opportunity to get into the mountains. Both kids learned to ski and I remember Pete and I dug out a snow cave somewhere on the slopes of Mount Rainier and stayed overnight in it. Again, we rarely let bad weather interfere with our adventures. After a couple of years in Washington State I had completed my obligation to the Navy and we were considering staying there and joining a local private medical practice. Instead I received a call from a senior officer (again it was Dr. Bob Higgins) advising that they needed a family physician at the medical clinic in the US Embassy in London, but I needed to decide "right now". With my hand over the phone I quickly briefed Leigh on the situation and she agreed then that we would put our plans on hold and go to London. We were off again to Europe.

We put both kids into British schools but neither of them were happy with the rigid discipline. Peter especially was not very good at staying in his seat. Eventually we transferred them to the American elementary school where Leigh worked as the school nurse. We enrolled both of them in etiquette classes, and learned quickly to our dismay that we just didn't have enough flatware and glasses on the table. The two kids just absorbed the culture and history however. We saw castles aplenty, gardens and parks, Scotland and Wales, the Hill country, the

Cotswold's and spent lots of time in London. I had regular hours and we lived about 45 min. outside of the city. It was during this time that Pete really got the travel bug. We visited Germany, Austria, France, Belgium and the Netherlands. I believe Pete really acquired his love of mountains in Germany. We went several times to Bavaria and skied at Garmisch. The Alps seemed to fascinate Peter. He could not stop talking about climbing this or that. Again traveling was a gift and especially for Pete.

About this time, I was done with my obligation to the Navy (again) and we were considering setting up a private practice. On one of our occasional trips back to Colorado to see family we stopped by at the minor emergency center in Castle Rock. As Peter grew we kept in touch with one of the nurse practitioners there and would occasionally send a picture or postcard. When we arrived at the center, who was there but Dr. Frank Martorano who had saved Pete's life, he was on-call and seeing some patients. He informed us that Swedish Hospital wanted to turn over the minor emergency center function to a group of family docs and asked if I would be interested. Swedish was willing to help with the costs of a new building and practice startup. This seemed like a tremendous opportunity to go home and Castle Rock still had very few medical doctors in 1986. To me it also seemed to fulfill the words **"I have a plan and a purpose for Peter".** We would go back and help the community that helped us so much with our son.

The next six years we built and operated a multispecialty clinic and urgent care medical practice in Castle Rock Colorado. The hours and commitment were all consuming. Julia put a voice message on our home phone, "Doctor and Mrs. Terbush are not here, they are at the clinic". Pete had an especially hard time with the local social scene at school. He was always good at wrestling kids his own size but too small for football or basketball. In addition his experiences made him a social outcast when he spoke about the things he had seen in Europe. This turned around in the fifth grade when Pete formed a climbing club and was able to get several of the other boys to join him. They climbed a number of local pitches and I helped them with some equipment. It was during this time that Pete and I discussed the importance of a proper belay. We practiced in Castlewood Canyon and Pete became confident that I would catch him if he fell. Eventually we switched and Pete had me on belay and although I outweighed him by almost 100#, he could stop me, (if he anchored himself). Pete would occasionally get in over his head, like the time we had to rescue him off of Castle Rock itself. He and a friend had climbed up the sandstone formation to a shallow indentation in the rock. Unfortunately the grip was marginal going up and he could not get enough traction with his climbing shoes to come back down. I don't remember how long the two boys were waiting up on the rock but eventually someone walked by below and the boys shouted for help. I got the phone call soon after at the clinic and with the help of friends at the Castle Rock fire department we went to the base of the rock and then climbed up to get the boys, a very humbling experience for Peter. When he graduated from Larkspur elementary school later that year he received the person "most likely to be Indiana Jones" award from his teacher.

During these years Pete and I were able to climb in the Colorado Rockies. He climbed his first 14,000 foot mountain or 14'er at age 10. Some Colorado kids summit these mountains at even younger ages. We then did winter ascents of a couple of 14'ers and went snow camping on skis. One particular trip on the 10th Mountain division trail system near Vail we spent the night in snow holes that we had pushed into the side of the drift with our "bivvie sacks" and sleeping bags inside. When he was 14 he was just old enough to participate in Colorado Outward Bound. This experience only added fuel to his passion for the mountains. Part of the course requires the students to spend a day and a night by themselves in the wilderness. He came back from OB more mature and confident. Soon after returning he had gotten in trouble with his mom over something he did and she said he was "grounded" and could not visit with friends. Peter somehow convinced her that if he climbed up Pike's Peak by himself that he would still technically be "grounded", and that is what happened. She took him to the base of the mountain and the following day she picked him up on the top of Pikes Peak and drove back down.

When Peter was old enough to drive a car his radius expanded considerably. Fortunately he hung out with good kids who also loved to climb and hike. Peter liked to telemark ski and became quite accomplished. Carving big wide graceful turns he had his knee almost touching his uphill ski, which required tremendous strength in his quads. He also developed a lot of upper body strength from climbing but was still very light, only about 130 pounds. He was "greyhound thin", someone said. He also took SCUBA lessons and got his PADI card. We went on a couple of diving trips in Mexico and the Caribbean and Pete enjoyed it immensely. We also went hunting together but Peter was never keen on shooting something. One time we shot and killed an elk and I believe it saddened him. We field dressed the elk and I explained the anatomy to him as we did so.

Fishing was not his sport either. He learned to play the trumpet and then got his braces, so he stopped. He was always a voracious reader. His real love was climbing however. He was going to school in Denver at the time and there was a rock climbing gym right next door where he built his arm strength and his skills. He was there almost every day.

About this time the stresses of running a rural family practice in an underserved area became too much for me. I had been called up as a Reservist for Desert Storm and spent three months in Bahrain away from family and my medical practice. Not a long time away from home (considering how frequently Army and Navy physicians are deployed now), but enough to cause significant disruption. Leigh was our clinic's office manager and she was ready to do something else when I returned from war. In addition my practice partners and I argued over money and so eventually I determined that this was not where we wanted to be long-term. Leigh had already figured that out long before I did! Because of our time in London I still had some contacts in the Foreign Service. This was the opportunity we were waiting for and we decided to "go for it". After a lengthy vetting process we were off to Washington DC for some more training and then were assigned to the US Embassy in Singapore. Julia went to college at

Denver University but Peter headed overseas with us again, for more adventures.

It was during our assignment to Singapore that Pete really came into his own as a climber. This was shortly after the Michael Fay incident where an American teenager was caned by Singaporean authorities for stealing traffic signs and other mischief. This made a big impression on Pete, but did not slow him down much. He was attending the Singapore American School (SAS) which allowed him to make friends with other kids who had had similar international experiences. These kids were smart and talented, SAS was highly disciplined and the campus was beautiful. In addition the teachers were hand-picked, it was a tremendous academic program. Peter's playground however was a nearby rock quarry called Bukit Timah (or Tin Hill) in Malay. There was a deep emerald green lake in the middle with sheer rock walls all around. The kids could leap 40 feet, or sometimes more, into the water. Pete really polished his rock-climbing skills in Singapore and soon found a new circle of friends who also enjoyed his passion. Pete put up a number of first ascents on various rock walls and pushed the limits of what Singaporeans think is permissible. He was also known for a number of "hare-brained" schemes. This is also where Peter learned to ice climb. I should explain...

Ever since a family vacation to the South Island in New Zealand, Pete had wanted to climb there. He read the classic book about mountain travel over ice and snow; first published by the Seattle Mountaineers in 1950, _Mountaineering: Freedom of the Hills_. He devoured it, cover to cover, and learned all he could about ice climbing. He then announced that he had a plan to visit New Zealand and climb Mount Cook that next year. Peter's plans and reality were sometimes far apart. I told him that he still didn't know how to ice climb, he didn't have any ice climbing equipment and there was clearly no ice here in Singapore. Also, he didn't know anyone in New Zealand and by the way, he had no money. Now ever since Peter was a little boy, and became fixated on getting a Millennium Falcon spaceship toy, he wouldn't give up on something he really wanted. He got a job waiting tables at a local restaurant and when he had enough money he purchased ice climbing gear from the REI catalog. He would then practice at the quarry on a very steep mud slope. With rigid boots, crampons and two ice tools he climbed the mud slopes again and again. When he became more confident he even climbed some of the tropical hardwoods in the area, not a good idea in Singapore. He would come home covered in reddish mud but pleased with himself.

Why we ever allowed him to go I do not know. His grandfather Al drove him to the Changi/ Singapore International airport and the conversation on the way went like this, "I can't believe my parents are letting me go do this", said Pete. "This is a really big deal right?" Grandpa Al replied "yes, a really big deal, I hope you appreciate this chance, they trust you". Pete flew into Christchurch New Zealand and went to a climbing shop that he had visited before. He put up a notice on the board looking for a fellow climber to go to Mount Cook. Once he had the "hook- up" he and his new best friend traveled to the area and began climbing ice. The weather was terrible, the boys spent most of their time in the tent and they never made it up Mount Cook, but had a terrific time anyway. Pete did not check in by phone with me the way I had asked him to, so I called a friend in the New Zealand military to look-in on them. He verified they were in the park and doing okay. Pete and his friend eventually ran out of time and food. He was late getting back to Christchurch and almost missed his plane. I think he became something of an inspiration to his classmates in Singapore though because they didn't really believe something like that could happen.

Another adventure I remember is when Pete climbed Mount Kinabalu, 13,435', in Borneo. At the time he was hanging with some other young men who were planning a Singaporean Mount Everest attempt, and these guys summited Everest in 1998, found on-line at www.everest.org.sg. As one of the training climbs prior to Everest for the team, they planned to go to Borneo and climb Mt. Kinabalu. Leigh and I had a conference in Hong Kong and we left Pete expecting he would climb with the team. He called us when he was leaving Singapore with his buddy Scotty and called us again several days later when he returned home. What happened was that the two boys chose to climb the mountain at night. They spent a couple of delightful days on the summit, mostly in the rain, and then hiked back to where they caught the plane home. I have a happy picture of Pete doing a head-stand on the summit of Kinabalu with one of his shoelaces untied, classic.

Pete and Scotty had several other adventures which frequently involved jungle thrashing. One time they hired a small boat to Tioman, an island in Malaysia, to climb the "Dragon's Horns" and then proceeded up from the beach in full Indiana Jones mode, with mud and cuts and scratches, until they reached the base of the climb. Just the approach was exhausting and after a few furtive attempts withdrew and made it back down to the beach. Reaching the summit was not always the goal, having a good time climbing was. Once Pete and Scotty rigged a Tyrolean traverse between two apartment buildings in Singapore and nearly got arrested. Pete also climbed up the side of our apartment building and grinning, came in over the balcony. One of the nicest websites about Pete was put up by Scotty as a tribute to their friendship, found online at www. supertopo.com. Again I don't know all of Pete's adventures in Singapore but I do know that he made some great friends that have somehow managed to stay in touch with me over the years. A couple of his friends continue to climb and lead expeditions on big mountains.

Peter had always wanted to climb in the Himalaya so he bugged me about it until he finally wore me down and my full attention. He had already been to Nepal and Bhutan with his high school, (my school by contrast would go to the Denver Museum of Natural History). He could not go with the Singaporean Everest team as he was not a Singaporean national. When Pete graduated from high school and before he left for college we scheduled a trip to the Garhwal Himalaya in Northern India. Pete and his friend Justin Lean picked the mountain with the help of a guiding service in New Delhi. I was the reluctant partner and meal ticket. We were assigned an Indian liaison officer whose name was Mohit. We also had a driver, a cook and a high-altitude porter as part of our team. Those readers who have been on a Himalayan adventure will find the following very familiar. Driving north from New Delhi we crossed the plains and into the foothills near to where the Ganges River exits the mountains. Our driver, who seemed to be intent on setting the world record for speed on these narrow mountain roads, finally got to me. I kept the expedition's money in rupees with me at all times and would parcel that out as we went along. I threatened to withhold his pay and cigarettes and with the help of our high-altitude porter translating, he finally slowed down. We saw evidence of cars and trucks which had careened down the mountainside, frequently. Finally we reached the little hamlet of Gangotri where we met up with the rest of our porters. We had picked a very modest mountain but plenty big enough for us. We were the only ones who had a permit for the Valley that summer, we did not see another party for the next two weeks.

Our goal was Peak Jogin 1, at 21,000 feet and change, it was a mere foothill "but hey, we were in the Himalaya and climbing a mountain!" We climbed up the valley to the west of Gangotri with our band of porters until reaching the beautiful lake, Kedartal, at the base of one of the most magnificent mountains I had ever seen, Thalay Sagar, or "Quartz Mountain", at 22,651 feet. National Geographic has subsequently done a special article about that mountain and the severity of the climb. I really didn't know that rocks could do that, it looked like gravity couldn't allow it. Our mountain by comparison, Peak Jogin 1 could be ascended by a relatively gentle snow slope leading to an icy summit. We had to load carry a couple of times up to 18,500 feet and get our gear into position. Pete was just amazing. After the first day of load carrying, Peter had developed a high fever (102F) and had diarrhea. As he recounts in his climbing journal he was "shaking like a puppy". I put him on some antibiotics and by morning he was ready to carry loads again to 18,500'. We then set up in tents at our "high camp" and were ready for our summit attempt. Mohit, who was built more like a weightlifter than a climber, was the first to succumb to altitude sickness. Our high-altitude porter had to take him back to the base camp by the lake. And then we were just three; Justin, Peter and myself.

From there it was a battle against time and exhaustion, hip deep snow, dehydration and high-altitude. There were no real technical challenges until we got near the top. The actual summit peak was rimed over with windblown snow. Justin and Pete did a fantastic job of climbing up and over the last few dozen feet or so of near vertical ice. I followed on belay. Coming back down we found ourselves in whiteout conditions and just sat down for a while. Eventually conditions cleared and we found our high camp and spent the next 24 hours brewing up hot drinks and recovering. The following day we felt good enough to proceed on down and were met by our high-altitude porter on his way back up to meet us with a note from Mohit. The note said "because you were delayed I have sent a message to the US Embassy asking for rescue". I could not believe it. We then scurried down the slopes to base camp, to include a long (glissade) slide on a snow slope using our ice axes to control the speed. Coming into camp there was Mohit with a big smile and several bottles of water with Gatorade mix to welcome us back. I confronted him about the note and he replied, "yes, if you had been gone one more day I was going to send the message for rescue". All was forgiven and we celebrated an easy climb and a safe return. Only later did we find out the Gatorade had been made with water from the lake. Pete and I had diarrhea for months.

Because we were off the mountain so quickly we had some additional time to explore the area. We crossed over into the next valley and saw Mount Shivling and the Bhagirathi peaks. We could just see another party summiting Bhagirathi 3, in the binoculars. Pete and Justin made some quick climbs on the lower slopes of one these monsters, I was content to just take a break. Finally on the way down to the mouth of the Ganges River where it exits the glacier we saw Indian mystics, the Sadhus or wandering monks. These were the ones who could stay outdoors essentially naked in freezing weather, sleep on rocks, sleep on nails, control their pulse, etc., etc. They were just skin and bones and had assembled in front of them a number of penis shaped stones which they worshiped. We offered them some Snickers bars which they gladly accepted and ate but we had second thoughts and worried that the sudden calorie load of sugar and peanuts could kill them. There was also a constant stream of pilgrims ascending the trail with empty water bottles to obtain some water right at the source of the sacred River, for good luck.

We gave most of our gear away to the porters who came to say goodbye in Gangotri. Mohit got a couple of sleeping bags and our high-altitude porter a new parka. As we drove back down the tenuous one lane road we came up on a corner where a number of people were looking over a guardrail into the chasm below. Another bus loaded to the top with people and luggage had gone over the side and rolled approximately 600 feet, losing its passengers, contents and eventually the entire bus body. Only the frame and wheels remained together, upside down in the tops of trees far below. Some of the victims were attempting to clamber and crawl back up the hillside, but no one was climbing down from the road to help them. Peter and Justin rigged climbing ropes to the guard rail and rappelled down to help the injured. I was surprised at the eerie quiet when I made it down to where a number of the injured and dead were scattered. Only a few soft moans were heard as people lay on the side of the hill in the bright sunshine. Eventually we helped a number of people to gain the road but I believe nine died at the scene and another three died en route to the hospital. The bystanders did eventually take action but only after Peter and Justin had gone over the side to begin the rescue efforts. I could not have been more proud of those two boys. Later, at the airport in New Delhi, Pete was so sick and dehydrated from diarrhea that he could not stand up for any length of time. We knew that if you looked ill, the airline could bump you from the flight. Pete had never completely recovered from his earlier illness. I remember Pete draped over our gear bags and then quickly standing, trying to appear well enough to answer questions from the attendant to get a seat on the plane, where he could rest.

While we were still living in Singapore we had another great adventure, sailing in Thailand. Leigh and I had been taking sailing lessons and most of our lessons unfortunately included dodging around large ships anchored in the harbor. We were looking for the next step up in sailing and chartered a 37 foot sloop in Phuket, Thailand; tropical waters, palm trees, exotic islands, and our own (rented) boat. Now this was what we had hoped to enjoy when we started these lessons. Our daughter Julia and her new boy-friend Tom Dunlap (or TD) came to join us from the US. Pete came back over from Colorado as well. Peter had been up in this area before climbing and exploring this part of Thailand. He and his buddy Scotty had previously taken a trip to Krabi Thailand across the Andaman Sea from Phuket and had rented motorcycles to get around. Krabi is a major center for climbers, there are large vertical rock faces and just to the north there are a number of limestone fingers which come up out of the Andaman Sea and have been featured in a movie, (James Bond, The Man With the Golden Gun, 1974). At one point our freshwater supply on the sailboat ran low and we decided to haul in to Krabi to replenish, and take some showers.

Thailand was amazingly inexpensive back then and so we could rent a room of sorts with a shower for just a few dollars. After getting cleaned up we walked into the little town and were surprised to find out that Peter was very well-known in Krabi. People kept coming up to him, they called him by his name and told us how great it was to see him there. We were a part of Pete's entourage....I guess? I never did figure that one out. After some fantastic local food Leigh and I went back to the sailboat to sleep but the kids stayed ashore where there were fireworks, loud music, and a bonfire on the beach, all night long. They had a great time. The following day we headed the boat out to the Northwest to see those limestone fingers. Pete selected one he thought was promising and we threw our climbing gear in the dinghy and we motored over to the island. Pete had planned this out well in advance and so of course had his full complement of gear. We found that the way the limestone eroded it had extremely sharp edges and was making cuts into our hands and the rubber soles of our climbing shoes. After several hundred feet of climbing we made the top and could see our little boat anchored a short distance away. We looped a sling around the actual summit and clipped our climbing rope through a carabiner so we could put it after us as we descended. Unfortunately after making it about two thirds of the way down we could no longer pull the rope back through the carabiner, it had caught on the sharp rocks. We still lacked the beach by about 80 feet and because we had rappelled down another way we were blocked from climbing back up to retrieve our rope. About that time, hot, tired and thirsty, small red ants started dropping off the bushes onto us.

We were gone quite a bit longer than we expected and so Tom came back over in the dinghy to see what was wrong. We lowered a combination of vines, belts and slings and anything else we could find down to him and he attached one of the boat's ropes and we hauled back up. We rappelled down the last 80 feet, drank some water and headed back to the boat. Tom is credited with saving the day that time and several other times since. He and Julia were married in November 1999 and I really enjoy him as my son-in-law. That trip was formative for our family and we continue to love to sail together with our daughter's family. (Now our two grandkids are learning to sail and a sailing day is "the best day ever!").

Chapter 3
Conflict and Resolution

*"It filled him with a great unrest and
strange desires. It caused him to feel a vague,
sweet gladness, and he was aware of wild yearnings
and stirrings for he knew not what."*
– Jack London, The Call of the Wild

Soon after our Himalaya climb was complete, Pete went to back to the US to go to college in Colorado, where his declared major was geography. His real major was climbing and skiing in the nearby Rocky Mountains and he formed the first climbing club at the University of Colorado, Colorado Springs. He did not have good luck though with the "beater" car we gave him and it spent most of it's time parked, but that did not slow him down much. Pete continued to have what he called epics, trips that did not turn out exactly as planned. He would rough out a climb on the back of a napkin, call his friends, preferably one with a car, head out on a moment's notice and then squeeze every last minute out of the weekend to arrive back at class just in time. Peter was not feral, but pretty close. He definitely felt the "call of the wild". OK, maybe he missed a few classes.

One was a quick trip up to Wyoming to climb the Grand Teton. They launched from Colorado Springs. He and his climbing buddy from Singapore (Scotty had moved to the US) made a quick ascent up the peak, hampered only by the number of people on the route. After summiting and starting back down they waited a long time at a particular rappel where it was jammed up. They were late getting off the mountain. Below that in a steep snowfield they set up a snow bollard and used it as protection to down-climb. When they reached the end of the rope, they expected to be able to pull it back down to them, but it was frozen fast. They pulled and yanked until one of them had a bright idea, they would both take a running start down the hill and the weight of both bodies together on the rope would break it free. This worked, but the boys were now hurtling down the steep snow slope, attached to each other. The visual I have of this is like a "Slinky toy" going down steps, one would self arrest then get pulled off by the other. As the slope eased they both were able to get enough traction with their ice-tools, and Pete said when they stopped, "it was just a little bit above the moraine", (rocks pushed up by ice). The two now had to find their tent and stumbled around in the dark, among the boulders, until they were exhausted, so they pulled out the bivvie sacks and slept cold. They found their tent some 50 yards or so away in the morning.

Leigh and I had moved on from Singapore and were assigned to the Embassy in Athens Greece. After a year there in Colorado Springs, Pete moved over to Greece to be with us and continued to go to school, but online with University of Phoenix. What he liked about that was he could knock out several lessons at once and reserve the rest of the day for his real avocation, climbing. He continued to take advantage of his circumstances and explore the world around him. Pete met a number of new friends who were climbers. He and his friends chose to visit places like Meteora, again a place where they had filmed a movie, (James Bond, For Your Eyes Only, 1981). This is also where Peter got into paragliding or parapenting as they called it. For a Summer he and an older friend, (the famously no-good Chris) formed a business to assist German and Swiss tourists to "fly" parapents in Greece. Chris was from France, honest that is not why I didn't like him/ but he was my nemesis, I thought he was trying to get Peter killed.

The two boys had read somewhere about bungee jumping from a parachute, and were going to take it the next step. Bungee jumping is typically done from a bridge or tower, something a little more stable. Since a parapent was a lot like a parachute (a soft airfoil) they figured that this would work out also. Later they told me the "did the math", not likely.

Supposedly no one had ever tried this before, so that increased the desirability of doing it. They went to one of their favorite flying spots with a tandem parapent, Pete was on the end of the bungee, of course. They soared off the mountain, went some distance to be a sufficient altitude above the ground, and Pete jumped. The bungee was attached to Pete's ankles and he bounced back up toward the parapent, several times. DO NOT TRY THIS AT HOME! The shock loading on the parapent must have been tremendous. The nylon fabric and cords could not have been designed for this. Pete was the first to reach the ground and quickly struggled to his feet and Chris landed a short distance away. My only record of this stunt is the account they told me later and a single photo Peter took with his ankles in the air attached to the bungee cord going up to Chris who was "flying" the parapent far above. When I heard about this one, in our living room, I went ballistic and kicked Chris out of our house and told him to never come back. I was disgusted with the whole adrenaline rush thing, and told Pete so.

This was getting old. I was always a "make it happen", guy and was raised with a strong work ethic from my father and mother. In my view work included getting up every morning, strapping on a suit (or uniform), and spending 8 to 10 hours or more at a job and then coming home. Although I was not seeing many patients, I was still gone a lot. My job required me to travel about half of the work days to visit other Embassies in the region and so I did not see either my wife or son on a daily basis. Long gaps exist where I heard very little about what Pete was up to. Pete climbed extensively in the Italian Alps and then on up into the French Alps. By the time Pete left Greece after a year with us he had expanded his climbing log considerably and was taking less experienced climbers with him and "showing them the ropes". I should be grateful that he did not get into any trouble; drugs or worse, but I didn't see him making much progress towards a career. About this time we were invited to go on a trip to a very sacred place for the Greek Orthodox Church, Mt Athos.

Visiting there was a special gift and we only received permission because our good friend Vangelis had told them that we were Orthodox, "Lord forgive us," we are not. Athos was actually one of three peninsulas in northern Greece near Thessaloniki. There were no roads except right at the port, ostensibly no cars and no electricity. There were also no women allowed in any of the monasteries and allegedly no female animals, but this stretches belief. There were however a series of ancient monastery buildings that had been built back as early as the 1200's. The monks continued their rituals and prayers much as they had for almost 800 years. We hiked from one to another, often arriving right at dusk when the big gates were being closed for the night. We arrived at one particular monastery, the Serbian monastery, again late and we were soaked to the skin from rain. One of the monks met us and showed us upstairs to a couple of rooms and started a fire in the wood stove. We stripped off our wet gear and laid it around the room to dry. We ate some food and were getting ready to call it a day when Pete said I smell smoke. We headed back into the other room where a pair of trousers was smoldering on the wood stove. One of the fellows yanked it off the stove and that gave it just enough oxygen to burst into flames. Bits of flaming pants were all over the room as we rushed around to put out the small fires. Although the outside of these monasteries were stone, the inside was definitely not. I hesitate to think about the headline, "US Embassy group burns down the Serbian monastery".

It was also this time when I believe that Peter heard the gospel message in the clearest and most positive way. We would get up at 4 AM for prayers and then the worship service would continue for a couple of hours when we would catch a quick breakfast with the monks. Although this sounds severe we were transported back in time with the beautiful chanting and ceremony of the service. One of the monks was a physician from New York City and he claimed to have seen many miraculous things happen there, especially when the monks died. Another told us about how relics had been passed down through the centuries and were again involved in many miracles. The father superior (or whatever they call them), brought Pete and myself aside to tell us about God's love and Christ's sacrifice on the cross for us. He allowed Pete to ask as many questions as he wanted and then prayed with Pete for salvation. I believe that if he had not already done so, Pete committed himself to Christ at that point. I personally could not have imagined a more perfect scenario or place to have heard that message. Later on I received a beautiful letter from the physician we met, about Peter. If there ever was a place on this planet called holy, this Mount Athos is certainly one. Our friend Vangelis was a sick man but I did not know it at the time. He died from liver cancer about six months later and Peter helped him through the dying process in a very compassionate way, by visiting him at home and assisting me with his end-of-life care.

We bought another beater car in Greece, which was an embassy tradition. The deal was that an embassy family would sell you their old car for a very low price, say $500, with the idea that you would drive it for a couple years and sell it to another embassy family for about the same amount. This particular car, a 1970's white Toyota sedan, had been passed down several times already. The car was a real survivor and well-known to the embassy community. Cars continued to be a problem for Peter. Pete had a new climbing buddy Michael who seemed to be willing to scheme along. The two boys had decided they wanted to go ski mountaineering and chose Mount Olympus (9750'), further up the peninsula, for their destination. Pete borrowed our old white Toyota and the boys drove up to the snow line and hiked up from there so that they could ski out the following morning. I got a call from Pete the next day who said, "Dad, the good news is we're okay, the bad news is the white car is stuck in the snow".

What really happened was that while the boys camped out overnight, a snowstorm moved in and blanketed the area with the foot or so of fresh snow. The boys skied down to the car expecting to be able to drive out. Instead they skied down the entire road, about 10 miles until they could link up with the rail and took the train back to Athens. Over the next six months the white car became somewhat of a tourist attraction. When we saw it was almost completely covered with snow and hikers regularly walked past it on the way to a lodge a short distance above. In January Pete had an idea which was to attach a cable to the car and push the car over the lip onto the steep slope below and slide it down to where the car could be driven out. This crazy idea made just enough sense to engage myself and a friend from work. Following Pete we hiked up to the car and spent the night in a shepherd's cabin where we had to dig down though several feet of snow just to open the door. The next morning it was pretty obvious to me at least that there was no way we could move the car even a few feet and get it close to the edge.

So the car sat there until May when Peter and his (also no-good) friend Michael went back up to drive it out. They had borrowed my little red sports car, a 71 MG Midget, to get up there. I got another phone call which began, "Dad, the good news is we're okay"… but they had managed to wreck both cars. Michael who was not much of a driver had rolled the white car. The boys got it back on the road and pulled the right front fender away from the tire so that they could at least drive and steer. The windshield was broken as well as the right side passenger door glass. They had found a mechanic in the small town nearby who could help get the car ready for the long drive back to Athens. In his haste to get back home Peter had managed to back the little red car into a light pole bending the back bumper and pushing in the trunk. It was a two for one.

We did not see the white car for a long, long time, he kept it in a friend's garage while he attempted to repair the damage. Finally we gave him an ultimatum, "'bring the white car back no matter the condition, so we can at least use it". As I had mentioned it before the US Embassy community is pretty tight. When Pete drove the white car on to the embassy grounds most people to include the guards already knew what had happened. The windshield was repaired as was the passenger side window but the right front quarter panel was missing and you could easily look and see the engine and fan, the tire and suspension were completely exposed. Eventually both cars were fixed but we remember having to drive to the Athens airport to pick up my parents in the crash derby white Toyota.

This was during the period of time when our relationship changed. I believed that many of the things he was doing were irresponsible and reckless, but that I loved him so much and wished in a way that I could be so free, I was never very harsh. But our conversations about mountain climbing and his epics became tiresome to me. He was obsessed with the next great adventure and I was worried if he would ever complete school and get a job. Eventually it became quiet around our house and Pete knew things were different. He was still the happy guy and was working at the embassy and going to school online, enjoying life and looking forward to the next opportunity to be in the beloved mountains. This was when I tried to get him to enlist in the Army.

Because I was still in the Navy Reserves and was around military many times each week it was a natural for me to discuss Pete's future with my friends. The Army attaché particularly was helpful and he also had an attractive daughter that I believe Pete noticed. The attaché and I decided that Pete would travel up to Germany to meet with the recruiter and begin a three or four year stint. Pete and I had discussed the proud history of the 10th Mountain Division which had been based originally in Colorado at Camp Hale. I also spoke with him about Special Operations or completing Ranger school and the many challenges associated with that. He could have joined the Army and finished his training, about the same time as the 9/11 attacks. I can only believe that he would have been involved in the response to Afghanistan, or elsewhere.

Instead we received a fairly bureaucratic response from the recruiter. Although accurate, it was discouraging that there could be no guarantees for Pete that he would end up in any particular unit or have the opportunity to pursue any particular special training. At that point, and admittedly with a certain lack of enthusiasm on my part about the process, Pete dropped it. In retrospect I think Special Operations or Ranger training was a bridge too far. Pete could have been a pretty good medic, he took a real interest in field medicine, and became an EMT later. There are many jobs in the military he could have done but they all required giving up his freedom, at least temporarily. My attempts to engineer Peter into this or that career were completely unsuccessful. He was studying a variety of subjects but not focused on any particular one. We discussed teaching as a path to a career but doubt that Pete could have been content, confined to a classroom. He liked geography and was pretty good as a result of his travel experiences. As time went on he settled on geology as a major and particularly the study of glaciers. Not a huge calling for glaciologists though. The real advantage however of taking classes online was that he could breeze through several lessons in one sitting and then head out the door to go climb.

He ran a marathon with almost no training. The US Embassy had put together a running club and a number of us, about 20, began training to run the Athens marathon. We were doing the run/ walk (Jeff

Galloway) method where the goal was just to complete the 26 miles and not necessarily look for any time. We all hoped to come in at around four hours or a little better. Each week we would train harder and on the weekends go out for a long run and build endurance. We were about the 12 to 15 miles mark when Pete decided to join us. He ran the first time with us in his approach shoes until we went and purchased some real trainers. Afterwards, he joined us for the long run each weekend until we were up to 20 miles. The 1998 Athens marathon was important to the Greeks because it was the Centennial of the rebirth of the ancient contest and the beginning of the modern Olympics. We did not try to duplicate the famous run of the original marathoner but instead the route took us through the city of Athens and finished in the marble stadium downtown. Pete finished way ahead of me and as I plodded along, he purchased snacks along the way from street vendors, waved and smiled and did a cartwheel in front of the US Embassy staff near the finish line. Jeff Galloway himself showed for the party afterwards.

Pete was pretty much "the dude" for the last few months he was in Athens. I let him borrow the red sports car and he would drive around with his long curly reddish hair blowing in the wind. He met a nice girl named Sophia and got into the Greek culture and schedule of the locals. In Greece people get up late, take a long lunch, frequently go home in the afternoon and then return to work late into the evening. Dinners will often start about 10 PM or later. Pete would come home in the wee hours or occasionally the sun was already up. He knew his way around the city and made do with enough Greek to converse with the locals. His job at the embassy did not take up so much time that it interfered with his climbing. He and I didn't really talk too much back then, I'd hear snippets of his adventures from time to time, when he chose to share them with me. It irked me that I could not see where he was headed with all this. Pete was 20 (almost), and still living at home, so I got on him about it and pressed him to make something of himself. I guess maybe I was a little jealous of his freedom also. I don't remember when Pete left but there was no celebration.

He went back to college in Colorado, this time Western State in Gunnison. Turns out this was even closer to mountains and ski areas, Pete was back in his element. Leigh and I were then transferred to Pretoria South Africa and I had a chance to travel extensively as a part of my job. We were separated from Peter and Julia by many time zones and were hoping that they would come to visit and get to see some of the incredible sights, sounds and smells of

Africa; game parks, mountains, rugged sea coasts, the wine country and a real diversity of cultures. South Africa remains our favorite overseas posting. Peter was planning to visit us in South Africa that summer of 1999 and we had talked about climbing Mount Kenya while he was with us. I really thought that was a little ambitious, I was out of shape but Peter had made plans, talked it through, and was intent on getting his ol' Dad up a big hill one more time. I had also decided that this would be the time when I would focus on Peter to get his life organized and headed toward a career that would pay the bills. Peter would be my "full-time project" until I got him straightened out. He told me instead he wanted to be a mountain guide and he needed to climb in "the Valley", Yosemite Valley. He was already climbing difficult aid routes in the Black Canyon of the Gunnison River and occasionally spending the night on the cliff face itself. The rock there was often rotten and he was looking forward to clean rock in Yosemite. We were headed toward a clash of wills.

He had wanted to climb in Yosemite for years. I had always been reluctant to encourage him to do so because I was afraid. I didn't know exactly the reason, but Yosemite frightened me. Why Pete wanted my permission to go there I'm not sure about that either, he rarely asked my permission to do anything. He said, "Dad, Yosemite is the real Mecca for climbers and I need to do it, if I want to be a mountain guide". He was going with some friends and expected to be there only a couple of weeks. Some of his buddies were already on the way. We had discussed how he would link up with his sister and then fly out from Los Angeles to South Africa to spend the summer with us. He left Gunnison Colorado and headed west. Pete then called us from Yosemite and told us he was having the time of his life, he was excited and sounded fulfilled and was living his dream. We told him that we loved him, and that was the last time we spoke. A night or two later Leigh and I woke up startled and worried. We had no indication anything was wrong and went back to sleep. The next day one of us dropped a beautiful Greek water pitcher outside by the swimming pool and I remember it crashed and broke into many pieces.

Chapter 4
An Heroic Finish

Greater love has no person than this,
that he would lay down his life for his friends.
John 15:13 NIV

The boys linked up in Yosemite and climbed a number of the big routes. Much of this was aid climbing where the person was not so much climbing the rock, but moving equipment upwards, standing in slings, being held up by a harness, and sleeping on a portable ledge. Everything they needed had to be brought with them or repeatedly hauled up from below. Some of these routes are now climbed free but I remember Peter loaded with slings and carabiners, nuts, and cams. Just the mechanics of hauling so much gear up and down was daunting. He climbed on one of Yosemite's most famous big walls, El Capitan, but was unsuccessful in reaching the top. There were gear problems and one of the ropes was shredded. Peter somehow felt responsible. After that he spent three days just hiking with a friend, Joe Kewin, and enjoying the scenery up above Tuolumne Meadows. Joe tells me it was one of the best trips of his life; no plans, beautiful scenery, physical challenges, he was pumped. They met an older climber, also called Pete, who traveled with them for the whole trip then disappeared. They also saw a mountain lion at close range. He and friend Joe came back from that hike tired but happy, and linked up with his friend Kerry Pyle for a short climb in the late afternoon, just above Curry Village and just below Glacier Point.

As was described in **Climbing Magazine** September 1999, "Terbush (belaying) and Joseph were on the ground when an estimated 150 to 200 tons of granite suddenly cut loose from approximately 1000 feet above. Kerry, leading some 60 feet off the ground, looked up to see car sized boulders careening down the slabs. As granite exploded all around them, Joseph fled the onslaught, and Peter Terbush boldly stood his ground belaying while Kerry attempted to place an anchor. Miraculously both Joseph and Kerry survived with minor injuries, but Terbush, 22, (sic) of Gunnison Colorado was killed instantly".

Shortly after the incident Kerry wrote, "With the heat of the day dissipating, and some cold refreshments in us, we decided to take advantage of the time left and climb "Mr. Natural" even though Pete and Joe are weary from their recent adventure. We hiked with enthusiasm to the base of "Apron Jam". Comically, Pete and I began racking up at the same time for the first pitch. After a quick game of paper, rock, scissors, I win the lead and finished racking up. I say, "On belay?", and Pete replies "belay on, climb when ready". "Okay, I'll try and hurry" I say. The climbing is easy for me and after placing "pro" about 25 feet up, I continue lay-backing the corner system. Two more pieces of gear find me just shy of the belay. Suddenly, a sound all too familiar to me resonates in my ears. I remember the wet slab avalanche that pummeled me on the north-face of the Grand Teton earlier this year. What's going on, there is no snow above me, and I'm in Yosemite? My mind races for answers, realizing that it is not snow making the noise, but rock!

Kerry continues his narrative, "There is no time to even cry out as an ocean wave of dust covers me making it very difficult to breathe. I can hear huge boulders smashing against the wall only a few feet away. One rock hits me square on the helmet and I feel nauseous and faint. Pain throws my free arm over my skull. I feel a warm liquid running over my face and down my arms and back. The slide is far from over and I go numb, waiting for the next rock to kill me. Time stops and I think of Pete and Joe below. Branches and scree fill up my shirt and chalk bag, and the blood on my face is thick with granite and dirt. I can see nothing and hearing is funneled through a ringing tunnel. "Pete! Joe!", I yell as loud as my lungs can muster, "hey are you guys all right? Pete! Joe!", no response… silence, listen. Then Joe answers back, "I'm here, where's Pete?" We both began to holler for Pete and there's no response. I tried to pull up the lead line but it was locked solidly in Pete's belay device. It was obvious that most of Pete's weight was pulling at my harness. "Joe, you have to take me off belay". He pries Pete's brake hand from the rope and unscrews the locking carabiner, his limp body falling into the open arms of his dear friend. For a second time I try to pull up the rope, but it is embedded under the freshly fallen stone. Joe pushes and pulls rocks off of it until I have enough rope to reach the ground. Rappelling down to Pete I instinctively clean the pitch, hollering good cheer to my companion below. "Stay with me Pete, help's on the way, you're gonna' make it man, come on Pete, answer me". I fall to my knees and scramble over toward him. Immediately I see the massive trauma to his head and grasp the unimaginable. A shaking hand searches for any kind of faint pulse, but there is nothing. Screaming at the top of my lungs, I yell questions and profanity into the sickening cloud of dust. I can hear Joe yell up from the valley floor "don't look at him", but my eyes are transfixed on my friend's beaten figure. He looks strong and brave, his belay hand still clutched at his side. It looks as though he was not at all afraid of death. Instead, he was only concerned about keeping me, the leader, as safe as he could. Taking his belay device off the rope, I grasp it in my bloodstained hands. I realize that my friend and partner had just saved my life. If he had jumped, run, or let go of the belay, I would've been pulled off the face or possibly fallen to the deck."

Park rangers and search and rescue personnel hurried to the scene. Because of the danger of additional rockfall they chose not to retrieve Pete's body for another 24 hours. Joe and Kerry were both seen at the clinic in Yosemite and their wounds were sutured but neither had significant injury. People on the Valley floor who witnessed this fled in terror as the dust cloud engulfed Curry village. Joe told me later that Pete could have run away, he did lean into the rock face to try and avoid being hit, but he never let go of the belay. He stood there and took it. Where Joe had been sitting was now covered with a huge boulder. Autopsy results showed that Pete's left arm had been broken but that a massive injury from the rock shrapnel blasting in every direction hit him directly in the back of the head and killed him. The rockfall itself lasted less than a minute but I'm sure for the three young men it seemed much longer. The area was closed off to climbers at that point, one of many times to come.

I received a call in Pretoria South Africa from my boss in Washington DC about 24 hours later. The Park Service had some difficulty finding us. My boss told me very quickly that there had been an accident in Yosemite and that someone from the Park service was going to call me in a few minutes. Shortly after that a Yosemite Park Ranger called and explained in some detail what had happened. He called Pete a "hero" and said, "He did exactly what he was trained to do, he maintained a proper belay". The other young men were okay he said, and Pete's body was being kept in Merced California. He did indicate that an autopsy would be conducted but I don't remember if it was a requirement or not. Either way it did not matter. Peter was gone and only his bodily tent remained, we now just needed to go to Yosemite, and fold up his "tent", and bring it home.

Because we were so far away it took a couple of days for us to get back to the United States and get up to Yosemite. Before we left, our church in South Africa rallied around and we had members from the congregation come to visit us. Our pastor particularly was very compassionate and empathetic; he had seen much violent death. On the way over we had plenty of time to contemplate what had just happened. The flight from South Africa to the US is one of the longest in the world. On board, by design or chance, there were a group of Orthodox Jewish rabbis coming back to the US as well. I engaged with one Rabbi about ritual care for the departed. He explained the Jewish tradition of a rapid burial but understood that there were many circumstances where this could not be immediately accomplished. Both Leigh and I were able to sleep some on that flight and we remember being comforted by spiritual "Praise" songs in our minds, in our dreams. Our friends from Colorado had already made it to Yosemite and particularly welcome was my friend Tim Ralph who was also my pastor and prayer partner from our time in Castle Rock

The mortician had done a good job of putting Pete's head back together. He looked strong, his chest was filled out, his back was straight, his shoulders were broad and his waist was narrow. I kissed him and took a couple of minutes to form a memory, then moved on to allow others to come see him. His mother had brought with her a T-shirt she had purchased for him in Australia. It read "Ayers Rock, Hard Rock and No Café". The young men had woven a section of climbing rope into what looked like a short staff and that was placed in his left hand. There was a nylon webbing sling over his shoulder. Pete was then cremated with his climbing boots on. These were the tools of his trade. We had decided that because we were still so unsettled we would take his ashes back with us to South Africa. We were presented later with Pete's ashes in an oak box and the scene of Yosemite Valley and the Chapel carved into the front. It was surprisingly heavy.

Our friends in Colorado had made arrangements for a memorial service back in Castle Rock. Pastor Tim led the service according to the program and his son Jesse, a friend of Pete's, had put together a memorable video of Pete's life put to music. It was a very unusual funeral service though. The small church was packed and then people from long ago turned up unexpectedly. Peter's nurse Bobbi from the NICU was there. Dr. Frank Martorano who had skied down that night and saved Peter's life at the minor emergency center, also came to the service. Pastor Tim then opened it up to the group, and many people spontaneously came to the front of the Chapel and said a few words. We celebrated his life and tried hard not to be sad. My brother Tom, a strong Christian, finished his eulogy with the words, "way to go Pete!" We then went a couple of miles away to the family property where we had built the cabin 21 years before. A group of us walked to the top of the grassy hill and placed a wooden cross made of redwood in the ground. Carved into it were the words "no greater love has any man than to lay down his life for a friend, John 15; 13. We said a prayer. A red tail hawk did a flyby.

PART TWO

SUMMIT IN THE ROCKIES

Chapter 5
"Servant Leadership, the basics"

"...in humility, consider others better than yourselves.
So look out not only for your own interests
but the interests of others". Philippians 2; 3, 4

When Matt Tyler, then director of the Wilderness Pursuits program at Western State Colorado University (WSCU), in Gunnison Colorado, met Pete in 1998, he was incredulous. "How could this young guy have done all the things that he said?" Pete was not bragging, he was only hoping to get a job. When he rolled out his climbing photo album Matt said, 'I could tell he was the real deal".

The original concept for the Peter Terbush Memorial Leadership Summit was put forward in August of 2001, by Matt. The "Summit" was to be an annual event to promote the concept of "leadership in service to others". The target audience would be student leaders of college and university-based outdoor programs. Matt was a former Outward Bound instructor and knew a lot about the formative aspects of time spent out of doors. The announcement of the first Summit was initially sent to colleges in the western United States but since has opened up to colleges throughout the country. It was specifically aimed at students with a "love of the outdoors" and who wanted to become mountain guides, like Peter did. Since then, the students have often been further along in their careers, some with advanced academic degrees and many who are leaders of University-based Outdoor Leadership programs themselves. The summit has as its core DNA, the story of Peter's final sacrifice in Yosemite.

From the beginning, the Summit was designed to teach technical skills (rock climbing and moun-taineering) to volunteer student staff, similar to Wilderness Pursuits. The technical skills curriculum is what first appealed to most students but aware-ness of the DNA within the Summit caused them to wonder "is something else going on here?" It began with a leadership training symposium and then the students went immediately to the field for six days in the high Colorado Rocky Mountains. The Summit motto initially described as "leadership in service to others", soon became shortened and focused to the two words "servant leadership" as put forward by Robert Greenleaf. This theme also formed the basis of nightly discussions in the skills training groups while students were in the mountains. The teams explored the concept that "we are true leaders as we give of ourselves in the service of others, ideally through repetitive giving, which forms the basis of true leadership".

Robert Greenleaf (in 1970) coined the phrase **servant leadership** and launched a quiet revolution. The term servant and leader may seem contradictory but he brought those terms together in a new and meaningful way. Quoting from _The Servant as Leader_, Greenleaf wrote that "The servant leader is servant first. It begins with the natural feeling that one wants to serve, then conscious choice brings one to aspire to lead. The best test is: do those served grow as persons? Do they while being served become; healthier, wiser, freer, more autonomous, more likely themselves to become servants? And, what is the effect on the least privileged in society; will they benefit, or at least not be further deprived?"

A number of other authors have written on servant leadership since. James A. Autry wrote in a book entitled _The Servant Leader_, the characteristics of the "leader as servant" are; to be authentic, be vulnerable, be accepting, be present and be useful. We took these concepts further to consider servant leadership as a model for mountain guiding. The mountain guide is servant and leader, both. He is a leader first because he knows the way ahead and leads his clients but a servant too. The guide must be concerned therefore principally about the clients' safety and welfare. The mountain guide needs to be out in front of the group both physically and mentally. To guide, he must anticipate; danger, fatigue, hunger and thirst and loss of courage. He must also be open to recognizing moments of supreme beauty, of heartfelt friendship and the so-called "teachable moment" a phrase used by James Dobson of Focus on the Family.

Pete was known for being a great encourager of others. He constantly had positive statements for his climbing partners and students. He seemed to have an uncanny sense for knowing when another person was about to lose their courage. He would shout "good move" or "just a little more". His classic line, "good skills" is the name of a new climbing route in the Black Canyon of the Gunnison. Pete would famously get up early at a camp site and make hot drinks for others. This too became associated with his particular brand of servant leadership. Friends remember him as self-sacrificing to a fault. Pete would care more about the experience of an individual group member than if they were successful in finishing the climb. He would take risks but would occasionally back away from a particular climb if it "did not feel right". One of Pete's last climbs was on a route called Tangerine Trip on the face of

Yosemite's El Capitan. Pete may have rigged a haul line improperly and this shredded one of the ropes needed to bring gear up to the climbers. His partners, for whom summiting El Capitan was the goal, were critical. Pete took the blame and the responsibility for "dorking up" the climb. Getting home safely was the goal now, and they did.

This brings us to the epic story of Sir Ernest Shackleton. We spend a lot of time at the Summit talking about servant leadership using the example of the expeditions of Antarctic explorer, Sir Ernest Shackleton. Shackleton's story of endurance and survival became thematic for the Summit in Gunnison. For most Summit students Shackleton is already a familiar name. Eventually we began to send out a book about Shackleton's leadership techniques, _Shackleton's Way_, Morrell and Capparell authors, to our students in advance. Shackleton's last epic adventure in Antarctica beginning in 1914, and lasting almost 2 years, has become an archetype for servant leadership principles. For those unfamiliar with this story, an extended synopsis follows below.

Shackleton has been described as a successful failure. He never managed to make his goal of setting foot at the South Pole, he lost his ship, his finances were in disarray, his family suffered from neglect, he had health problems, *and for decades his reputation was overshadowed by others such as Scott and Amundsen. He has now been recognized however as perhaps the greatest leader of a small group of men, of all time. Shackleton had already been to the Antarctic twice before. His first voyage was with Capt. Robert Falcon Scott (1901-1904) and ended for Shackleton when he became ill and was sent home. His second expedition the so-called Nimrod expedition (1907) carved away at the unknown continent and led future explorers on the way South. Shackleton's group came within approximately 90 miles of the South Pole but then turned back realizing that they had outdistanced their food supplies. Unlike Scott who in 1912 lost his own life, and that of some of his team due to starvation, Shackleton focused on "bringing them all home".*

After months of planning and fundraising, Shackleton and his small crew made it to the whaling station on South Georgia Island, December of 1914. The expedition's ship was named __Endurance__ which was from the Shackleton family motto" by endurance we will prevail". He was advised at South Georgia that it'd been a particularly cold season and that the icepack extended much further north than was typical. However Shackleton believed he could travel down the eastern edge of the Ross Ice Shelf and make landfall in order to set up his camp and winter over. When he could make no further progress south, the ship became set in the ice "frozen, like an almond in the middle of a chocolate bar" and the epic adventure began, (Orde-Lees journal).

Shackleton had chosen an unusual crew; a core group had already been tested in the Antarctic but some were brought for their technical or professional skills. There were men of both high and lower social class. To the greatest extent possible Shackleton treated them all equally. As winter progressed and turned to spring the Endurance was crushed by movement of the icepack. He famously said "our ship and stores are gone, it's now time to head home". It's hard to understand how completely isolated these men were, but with Britain involved in the Great World War and no means of communication, no one knew where they were or their status. If there was to be a rescue they would have to do it themselves.

They had salvaged as much food and supplies as they could reasonably load into the three lifeboats; named the Dudley Docker, the Stancomb Wills and the James Caird. Shackleton made every effort to keep the crew together and in good spirits. The patterns they had established during the long winter before had bonded them together and established Shackleton's position as "the boss". The team made several forced marches, pulling the boats through the ice but then finally, exhausted, set up camp to wait as the ice flow drifted slowly to the north.

The conditions were terrible, constantly wet and cold, the men were on short rations. Shackleton would make the rounds from tent to tent and send hot drinks for all if he found any individual who was particularly suffering from the cold. This gesture spared that crewmember any embarrassment. As the pack drifted slowly north, it melted and their floating home broke up beneath them. Forced to abandon the ice and take to the three lifeboats they made for Elephant Island, still deep in the icy southern seas.

Thus began the most famous part of the story, the open ocean boat journey, 800 miles back to South Georgia Island through the worst seas in the world. Shackleton and five companions set out in the James Caird, a 22 1/2 foot life-boat, on April 24th and made South Georgia on May 10th. But their troubles did not end then, they had been forced to land on the opposite side of the island from the whaling station. A mountain range as high as the Alps, and completely unexplored, lay in their path. Using equipment from the ship and putting screws down through the bottom of their boots they fashioned enough climbing gear to begin their trek. Shackleton recounts that on occasion they seem to be in the company of an additional climber or guide, to help them through the most difficult parts. After an extraordinary series of ascents and descents and at the limit of human endurance they managed to find the whaling station. The whaling station manager, who knew Shackleton, could not recognize him, from his appearance.

Four rescue attempts later, Shackleton made it back to Elephant Island to recover the rest of his crew. There had been no loss of life and the worst injury was some frostbitten toes. Soon after arriving back in England a number of the crew were involved in the Great World War (1914-1918) and were lost.

Shackleton's servant leadership principles were exemplified during this expedition to Antarctica. He had formed an extraordinary core of individuals and caused them to bond together during the long cold night. He was also an optimist and encouraged cheerfulness and recreational activity among the crew. He was fair and did not distinguish a person's worth by class or rank. Shackleton led by example, he was willing to help with even the most menial and difficult tasks and as a result, gained the respect of his men. He focused on the future and made memorable examples of commitment such as when he threw his gold watch and 50 gold sovereigns in the snow as it would 'slow them down'. Shackleton balanced caution and risk when he had to take the biggest risk of the expedition, the open ocean boat journey. He weighed the decision carefully and discussed it with his men. They kept to a disciplined routine and rolled up their sleeping bags each day, watching and waiting, because, "this may be the day the Boss returns".

Only once did Shackleton make an example of a crew-member. This was when the carpenter "Chippy" McNeish threatened mutiny. This was a defining moment for the crew and its leader. They understood that Shackleton must reassert his authority and he did so in such a manner that he was never effectively challenged again. From then on "Shack" kept Chippy close to his side where he could do less harm. Chippy was also the only one who was not nominated for a polar medal on return. Shackleton constantly had to make "mission critical" decisions, and he made enough good decisions that he got his men through. Enthusiasts tend to forget he did not always make the perfect decision but his crew would follow him anyway because he had led them successfully in the past. His authority was given from below not imposed from above.

Servant leadership inspires others. One of the frequent comments from participants in the Summit is that they were inspired to lead. Occasionally our students would also try to "out-servant" one another, practicing how to be "other" focused and attentive to needs of their fellow climbers. Instructors likewise look out for students who are falling behind, making poor choices or are less involved. The field work is exhausting and students are often tired, hungry and cold. These Servant Leaders in training are mostly civil to each other during the week and realize that all the team is experiencing roughly the same stress. The instructors have also taken on various Servant Leader characteristics. Some handle problems with humor, some call a safety "time out", others are more direct. One of the best examples of a Servant Leader is a person who is "selfless under pressure", that the essence of a person's character comes out when he/she is being "squeezed". It is that ability to still be true to your principles when your own privilege, comfort or even safety is at risk. I believe our instructors have those characteristics, and demonstrate them regularly.

Servant leadership of course has been discussed in the context of the example of the life of Jesus Christ. Many references are in the Old and New Testaments such as the "Suffering Servant" in Isaiah 53 or Matthew 23, where Jesus says, "The greatest among you will be your servant". As Christians we believe that how we live our lives and how we allow Christ to live through us, is eternally significant. Christ's example has special meaning for us as Paul says we are to 'imitate Christ", 1 COR 11:1. I'm convinced that the currency of the universe, the stuff that really counts, is self-sacrifice. It's a special form of love for another human being, Agape Love. This is not limited to epic adventures in the mountains. It's what a mom does when she stays up all night with a sick baby. It's when parents save for years so their child can go to college and it's what that child does by caring for an elderly parent. It's even in the little things that we do; holding doors open for someone or getting up early to make hot drinks. "Small acts of unexpected kindness", are also examples of Servant Leadership.

Chapter 6
"On the Rocks"

*Bumper sticker; "Never drive faster than
your guardian angels can fly".*

Peter had an amazing number of close scrapes. When we were climbing in India (Garhwal Himalaya, 1996) a rock the size of a washing machine tumbled down between us. Since we were on a long slope and there was no cover we just quickened our pace. Another time he was carried about the length of a football field in a "slough" avalanche, (Mt Quandary/Colorado, 14,265'). This was Pete's first winter ascent of a "fourteener". He was 12 years old and it was supposed to be an easy climb. We summited in good shape and stopped to have lunch while the warm Colorado sunshine began to melt the top layer of snow. He set off glissading, (sliding on your butt with an ice-axe) down the south facing slope and I followed behind. My weight must have triggered some of the sun-wet snow to start moving and gathering more snow as it proceeded, I saw that it was going to collide with my son. Pete heard my shouts and stood up, just as the mass hit him about knee deep. He was tumbled then "spit out" to the side. His hat and gloves went one way and his ski poles another. With mouth aghast, I watched the whole thing happen in perceived slow-motion but there was nothing I could do about it. The snow-slide then went over a drop-off and down toward the frozen lake below. When we got back home Pete and I did not share that part of the climb with his mom.

Years later, he told me about another avalanche on Berthoud Pass, on the way to Winter Park Colorado. He was back country skiing near the top of the pass and the snow broke away from under him and then gathered strength and speed. Apparently this set up quite a big slide below. Pete could have gotten caught up in it, but again only a scare. I sincerely hope there were no other cars or skiers below, he never heard of any. I'm pretty sure there were a number of other close calls that he never told his ol' dad about. My reactions when I did hear about them varied from surprise to humor to pride to frequently anger, and possibly accounts for why Pete did not bother to share all of his exploits with me.

One of the stories which explained a lot about Pete's character was mentioned in a story about a winter climb of Shavano Peak (14,229') in the Collegiate range in Colorado. He and a friend were doing a ski ascent of Shavano and got into some weather. Pete was the more experienced of the two and his partner became worried they were going to be stranded and have to spend the night. This was his friend's first big experience ski mountaineering. Apparently there were some gear issues as well. The friend relates that he was "really pissed off" at Pete because he seemed to be so unconcerned about the "peril" they were in. They seemed to be just swimming in the snow. Pete was still encouraging his friend about the route and kept on in his role as the teacher/ guide. They descended and eventually broke out of the weather, and Pete never took the opportunity to say "I told you so", or words to that effect. This was all just a part of mountaineering. It impressed his climbing partner so much that it was it was the one "Peter" story he chose to relate.

Peter actually lived under a rock for a while. This was when he was working at a casino in Cripple Creek Colorado. He and a couple of his buds had formed a company called "Dusty Angels", complete with business cards. They would clean up after the casino closed for the night and Pete said the boss would allow them to "keep the change" they found under the tables. "We made some pretty good money", he said. During this time Pete was sleeping rough, he would park his sleeping bag in a friend's yard and crash until his next shift. When I found him though he had managed to locate a shelter under some huge, building sized, boulders, but which had a tremendous panoramic view of the west side of Pikes Peak. His cave was open and airy and he even had a flat rock shelf big enough for his sleeping bag, tent and all the cooking equipment and other gear he had, which was laid around in typical Peter fashion.

I'd accused Pete of "plane crash" camping on more than one occasion, so called because his camp-site looked like an aircraft had crashed there. While he was living in Colorado I surprised him and climbed up to his camp-site where gear was strewn about the area. Guess he imagined that since there were no other people around, he could leave his stuff outside. However, I do believe he changed his pattern after an overnight snowstorm covered the area and he had to go searching for 'buried treasure". Pete was casual enough about his gear that he had things stolen several times. Once in Singapore he had left some of his rack (rock climbing nuts, cams and carabiners) at the bottom of a climb and "guess what?" it was gone when he returned. The only other time I can remember anyone stealing anything in Singapore except for the knuckle-head American boy Michael Fay who stole street signs and was "caned" for it in 1994. Pete also adopted a hitchhiker once known as "Sketchy Ed". Pete found him with his thumb out somewhere east of Gunnison Colorado. Ed came to live in Pete's dorm room at Western State, (not alloewed per the rules), and eventually became a regular fixture on campus. When Ed left unexpectedly some weeks to months later, so did a lot of Pete's stuff including his mountain bike. Pete was unfazed apparently and seemed more worried about my reaction than doing without a bike.

Another close call was about six months before his death in Yosemite, I believe it might have been a warning to Peter or just a presaging of events to come. Pete's Greek girlfriend Sophia came to visit him at Western State, (yes, she really came to visit the western slope of Colorado from Greece to see Pete), and toured around with him in the Rockies. She was also a climber, no doubt it's how they met, and she was a real beauty. She was a little taller than he was with dark hair and about five years older. Pete was taking her back over the mountains to Denver for her flight home to Greece. They were in Pete's ratty old Jeep CJ with the top off.....but no seat-belts on. A snow-plow came around the corner in the other direction and one of the two crossed over the middle. The plow hit Pete's Jeep and folded it up like a taco, it was totaled. Pete and Sophia were thrown out and into the snow. When the paramed-ics arrived they insisted in starting an IV in both of them, cervical collars, etc., and transporting to the Gunnison Valley hospital. After many x-rays both were determined to be fine. This was one of the very few cases I know of where staying in the vehicle probably would have been fatal. Would like to have seen that one through spiritual eyes, I think maybe the angels were giving each other the 'high five" on that catch. Pete got a ticket and State of Colorado wanted to charge us for damage to their snow-plow, but dropped it months later when they found out he was killed in Yosemite.

Selflessness is so strange that it becomes almost a liability. Pete was so un-self centered that I wanted to grab him by the shoulders and shake him some of the time. He took the blame once for a couple of friends who were in trouble with the campus police. Two of his female friends had another couple of guys over who were using drugs, marijuana I would guess. The guys had left paraphernalia behind in the girl's room when they left. At some point there was an inspection of the dorm rooms and the "bong" was found and campus and local cops became involved. The girls were scared and looked as if they would face mandatory discipline, parents would be notified and legal trouble which could ruin the girl's lives, or so they thought. Remember this was long before there was an "herbal health store" on almost every corner in Colorado. Peter, coming to the aid of the "fair damsels", told the police it was his stuff and took the hit, figuratively of course. We only found out later that he had to perform community service and faced other campus discipline, there are penalties for lying to the police. The girls were home free and were ever so appreciative, but puzzled. When one of them told me this story later, after Pete's death, she said, "I guess Peter was taught to protect women, and he did".

Peter must have struggled with his own particular anxieties, thoughts and fears although we never really got to the point in our relationship of just two adults sharing about life. I would have loved to hear Pete just express his thoughts and feelings to me, he may have tried when he was younger and I just missed it. I was always too busy being the dad, even when we were climbing together. Leigh said I was too focused on the goal and frequently missed the experience, (Leigh also said she did not enjoy climbing with me for that reason and was pleased when Pete was old enough to shoulder a pack). There was much I did not know about him, I still do not. I cannot remember Peter ever showing fear, ever. I believe he may have been afraid of me, and my disapproval. He was very likely in trouble or pain on occasion and I did not know it because I did not sit there and listen. He had an extremely high pain tolerance as we witnessed once when he was a boy. He reached into the dishwasher to grab something and impaled the muscle at the base of his thumb with a knife. He just looked at it while the blood streamed down on the floor. That relative insensitivity to pain was possibly related to his early beginning and the time in the intensive care unit, I do not know. He had some of the characteristics of other premature kids. A couple of times I did see him as his physician, when he showed up in the emergency room where I was working. He was riding on a miniature motor cycle, (cute little thing, 50cc or so), and flipped it. Fortunately he was wearing a helmet. He was brought in unconscious, carried by a neighbor who found him in the weed field near our place, with the motorcycle engine still running. I remember being very clinical about the whole thing as we laid him on a gurney, across the room from some other patient I was treating at the time. He was groggy and slowly recovered over ten minutes or so. We sold the motorcycle. Another time he was being pulled along behind an ATV in the snow on an inner-tube (typical Colorado kid stuff), when he, specifically his left ankle, hit a tree stump. He was again brought in by neighbors and he was in real pain this time. We got an x-ray and the orthopedic surgeon on call agreed we could just splint it and he would see him later on that day. I felt strange ordering a Demerol injection for my own son, but he soon had his relief.

Chapter 7
Legacy

"I have fought the good fight,
I have finished the race…" 2 Timothy 4; 7

Even as I write these few words I realize that my memories of Peter are fading. What really remains of a person after he or she is gone? Within a generation or two most of us are a footnote in a book, if that. Over the centuries people, families and entire civilizations have gone to extraordinary lengths to memorialize an individual. I'm quite sure that's not what Pete would have wanted me to do. He was a humble guy, who thought very little about himself and would be impatient to move on. There are a few things though that help me to remember what he was like. First are the numerous references on the Internet to Peter Terbush, some written by friends and many by people who never even met him. The Super-Topo website has a number of discussions which include Pete. Obviously the Leadership Summit in Gunnison and the Solid Rock Climbers for Christ found at www.srcfc.org have a lot of archived material. The *Peter Terbush Mountain Project* which describes the climbing in the Black Canyon of the Gunnison, is a great one and has pictures of the Terbush Tower and the route "Good Skills". Soon after the accident there were several articles in *Climbing Magazine* and *Rock and Ice*. Papers in California and Colorado also picked and ran the story. The *LA Times* reporter Eric Bailey has done several "fair and balanced" articles about Pete. There was a mention of him in the records of the American Alpine Association, his heroic actions, and his untimely death. He is also noted in the book <u>Off the Wall; Death in Yosemite</u>. David Lim mentioned Pete in a book called <u>Against Giants</u>, describing the successful Singapore Everest Expedition. There was also a book called <u>Triumphant Hearts</u> and it was dedicated to him, "Peter Terbush...a fine son, brother, man, friend... hero. He gave his life that another may live".

Tangible reminders of Pete include his memorial stone just outside the student center at Western State College in Gunnison. Made from the same type of Yosemite/Glacier Point granite, it was cut in Merced California and trucked to Gunnison. On it are the words that the Park Ranger told me that evening "he maintained a proper belay" and the Scripture verse most closely associated with Peter "no greater love has any man than this, than to lay down his life for a friend" John 15;13. Attached to that stone are the belay device that he was using when he saved Kerry and a locking carabiner which was attached to his harness. Kerry surprised us when he drilled the stone and put two rock bolts into place to permanently fix the equipment. Also, unknown to us was the climber's memorial in Yosemite that August. We don't really know what happened, but we heard they had a pretty good time. There was a climber's memorial in Singapore about the same time (August '99) organized by his friends there. His high school in Singapore, (The Singapore American School), placed a memorial stone on a wall of remembrance for students and faculty members. I have Pete's Bible and looking through the passages he underlined, I can see where he struggled in his faith. He also had a card in his wallet when he died, with the scripture, *Psalm 32; I will instruct you and teach you in the way you should go; I will counsel you and watch over you"*. My father keeps that one in his wallet now.

After he died, his friends "divvied up" his rack and some other gear. I'm told that is typical in the "gnarly rock-climber dude" culture and am pleased his stuff might still be used for climbing. I kept a few things myself; his tent and a torn up copy of Climbing Guide to the Yosemite Valley which he had in his backpack. I also have his "Harry Potter" type glasses. Of real significance and a surprise to me was the book he was reading in Yosemite, The Hero with a Thousand Faces, by Joseph Campbell.

The book discusses the enduring story of the hero, "the mono-myth", through cultures and time, from "Prometheus to Luke Skywalker". I am staggered by the coincidence. I put the book on his chest before he was cremated. I've since bought another copy and read it through, and marvel at Pete's choices in literature. I still have Pete's rock collection and of course his other books from home. I also have his climbing journal and some photo albums. Another couple of friends got his "parapent"/parachute hang glider and another one his bivvie-ledge. His one cousin got his watch and another one his pocket-knife. All these gifts were meaningful to both the giver and receiver.

One reminder of Peter is too mystical for me and I still get the shivers when I even think about the possibility. The day after the rockfall in June of '99 a helicopter with a USGS geologist aboard was featured in a photograph in the Sacramento Bee newspaper. Behind that helicopter was the massive scar on the face of Glacier Point with streams of water coming out from the back of the release point. The headline was "climber dies protecting friends" and in the byline from Yosemite Park spokesman Scott Gediman, "he sacrificed his safety for his friends, he held tight while he was getting hit". Soon after that article was written climbers in Yosemite began referring to the scar as the "white buffalo". Even in the earliest pictures you can make out the outline of a buffalo facing to the right. Nonchalant climbers have told me "oh sure, it's a buffalo all right". Kerry Pyle wrote an article about the events in Yosemite and titled it "The White Buffalo". The name stuck. As time passed it seems the White Buffalo scar has become even more pronounced. Recent photos taken from different angles continued to impress with its likeness. I like the idea but have trouble mentally and emotionally pulling all the pieces together. The white buffalo is a powerful symbol in Native American culture. Herds of buffalo used to roam in the Yosemite Valley. In the last couple of decades there are reports of white buffalo being born in the United States. All of the stories have one thing in common, that the arrival of a white buffalo portends significant events.

The ramifications of this part of Peter's story, are overwhelming. It makes me want to fall on the ground and cover my face and head. I am a scientist by training and by practice. I work daily with no-nonsense individuals who have awesome responsibilities. My own faith is one where I am open to the idea that God reaches out to us; to comfort us, to warn us, and to give us a hope for the future. But, have I ever seen where God carves the rocks? Over geologic time canyons deepened, mountains rose, and continents shifted. Earthquakes in Haiti, in Japan and elsewhere have caused shocking damage and loss of life. God carved the 10 Commandments in stone. God "breaks open the rocks" for thirsty people and He "makes the mountains smoke". Rocks and mountains are common themes throughout the Bible. "I lift up my eyes to the hills…..where does my help come from? My help comes from the Lord, the maker of heaven and earth", Psalm 121. I feel closest to my creator when I am in the hills and it is what I imagine Heaven to be most like. However, to be in the presence of something/ someone this much bigger than myself is devastating, "I AM" God says and we have no reply. But did God really cause those rocks to fall, or did God allow it? Did God spare my son from some other fate? Why was Peter at the base of the climb and not Kerry? Was it part of a plan created long before, to accomplish a purpose as was promised? I do not know but I am looking forward to a time and place where I can ask the question. God allowed his own son to die for us. He knows the end from the beginning.

Chapter 8
More Than We Know

"And therefore as a stranger give it welcome.
There are more things in heaven and earth, Horatio,
Than are dreamt of in your philosophy".
Hamlet/ Shakespeare

One of the things we love to do as a family is to go sailing and a lifetime dream of mine had been to become a "blue water sailor" and cross oceans. When the time came for us to leave South Africa we were fortunate enough to be assigned to the US Embassy in Buenos Aires Argentina. Because of the exchange rate, sailboats of high-quality were being made in South Africa and were relatively inexpensive. After some searching we found a boat still in the factory which had never been completed. It was meant to be an escape boat for a South African family who fully expected that their country would go up in flames during transition to majority government. Since that never happened, (I believe in large part due to the forgiving quality of churches in South Africa), the couple lost interest in the boat and it was never finished. She was a 39 foot cutter rigged sloop with center cockpit and a skeg-hung rudder.

She was overbuilt for South African waters; the standing rigging, cleats, sails, mast and boom were heavy and constructed for storms, not racing. The cockpit drains and several bilge pumps (automatic and manual), would keep her afloat even if she took a large wave. Hand-holds and plenty of places to clip in a harness could keep a sailor attached to the boat. There were numerous other custom built safety features. She had a 13 1/2 foot beam and six-foot draft; she was heavy, beamy, relatively slow and stable. She was built for crossing oceans and was very forgiving. We would scare ourselves many times but the boat never scared us. We added some electronics and over the next 12 months honed our skills in Table Bay off Cape Town and along the stormy west coast of South Africa. We named her the "Blue Peter" after the old British signal flag "P" or "Papa" which meant "we're headed to sea today" and of course after our son. Her sister boat called "Rotary Scout" had recently done the Cape to Rio crossing with a number of Boy Scouts as crew. If they could do it hopefully we could do it too! Another of the same series had circumnavigated. The boat's builders, Eric Nel and his son Etienne were with us during the whole process of getting "Blue Peter" ready for sea. In fact, Eric was willing to sail with us to South America, perhaps it was to go along and make sure we didn't screw up too much. Eric unfortunately was felled by a blood clot to his lungs approximately 3 months before we planned to set sail. I often imagined that Eric was with us during our journey in spirit.

Peter also was with us on that crossing in many ways. There was more than one occasion during our sea trials when I prayed out loud "Lord give me the courage of Peter", right before I had to do something risky. During the crossing itself I thought often about Pete, especially during the long night watches and believe I felt his presence. About mid-ocean we laid a wreath on the water in memory of him, (and Eric). We carried Pete's ashes with us on the boat. We made landfall in Rio de Janeiro Brazil after 28 days on the water. Another five days brought us to the mouth of the Rio de la Plata and then up the channel to our new home in Argentina. As we pulled toward a mooring at Yacht Clube de Argentino in Buenos Aires our engine quit and could not be restarted, although it had never caused us any problem before. We drifted without power or control onto the mooring and out of the darkness came a solo sailor to tie us up and give us a lift to the dock. His name was Angelo.

A couple of years later my friends and I were invited to climb Aconcagua, the tallest mountain in the Americas, with an Argentine Army team. Part of my personal mission was to also place some of Peter's ashes at the top. We had terrible weather and ended up not making the 23,000 foot summit but instead made some terrific friends in the Argentine Army. When we arrived back at base camp I shared with the Argentine leader about Peter's story and my other mission. (I had not mentioned anything about Pete before or during the climb). He was entirely moved by the story of self sacrifice and committed to me then to go back and place Pete's ashes at the top. There is a letter that he wrote to me, translated from the Spanish.

"Dear Sir; is with utmost pride and satisfaction that I write to you today to inform you that both your request and my promise were accomplished on February 18, 2001 at 2:25 PM. The ashes of your son Peter are now resting forever at 7000 meters of altitude on the highest peak of the American continent. With this letter I am enclosing the photograph which shows the urn I received (from you) placed at the foot of the cross that marks the summit of the Aconcagua Mountain. Weather conditions were not favorable and we thank God for blessing our efforts and allowing us to arrive safely. In addition to the massive amount of snow and ice we encountered, the strong winds made the climb to the summit extremely difficult and exhausting. The wind chill factor registered –50°C. Upon reaching the summit I focused on the task

at hand and separated myself from my companions, seeking the intimacy required by my mission. After saying a prayer for your son, I opened the urn, and standing at the edge of the imposing South wall, I spread his ashes towards the strong and cold wind, which in enveloped the summit. It was a moment of profound emotion, and although I had never met your son Peter I feel sincere affection for him. God gives very few, fortunate men, the opportunity to choose their own deaths, and I strongly believe that there is no higher glory than the one of giving your own life for a friend. I also believe that the split-second in which your son made that decision was supported by his belief in life, and the upbringing he received. Sir, I bid you farewell with the most sincere realization that this mountain soldier has completed his mission to the best of his abilities.

"The mountain unites us"
Capt. Claudio Rossini,
Eighth Mountain Climbing Company,
"The Cazadors", Argentine Army"

We also had the opportunity to visit Antarctica as part of a scientific and adventure tourism cruise. I went as ship's doctor aboard the M/V "Orlova", an ice strengthened ship which went from the southern tip of Argentina to the Antarctica Peninsula. As a part of the crew my wife as the ship's nurse and I had the duty to go ashore at each of the dozen or so landing sites in Zodiacs ahead of the tourists, to help establish landing sites. One of the locations, appropriately called Paradise Bay, was one of the most spectacular places I had ever seen. Leigh and I pulled apart from the rest of the crew and allowed some of Pete's ashes, which we had brought with us, to disperse in that beautiful location. Again we felt Pete's presence, (although we also felt a little guilty about leaving anything ashore).

In 2003, while we were sailing from Argentina back to the United States on the "Blue Peter", I remember feeling Pete's presence very acutely. We had a young crewmember on board, Guillermo, about Pete's age, who had traveled with us from the beginning of the trip. He and I talked about Peter, his life, and his sacrificial death. This seemed to profoundly affect Guillermo's thinking. We were about to cross the equator and were approximately 100 miles east of the mouth of the Amazon River. So massive it is the flow from the mighty Amazon that we could even see some change in the water that far out. That was when "night bird" came to visit. He was a seabird, probably a Sooty tern, and spent the night with us sitting on the radar cover. He was gone during the day but then came back again at night. He did this for two or three nights. We crossed the Equator near midnight and recorded it in the boat's log. Granted sailors are superstitious but having a bird ride along with you is supposed to be a very good thing. With night bird along I took heart and imagined Peter being there in spirit with us as we "crossed the line" and achieved this milestone in sailing.

Peter Terbush, 1995

Best buddies; Peter and Scotty

The Dragon's Horns, Tioman Island Malaysia

Climbing a new route in Singapore

Mt Cook National Park, New Zealand

Himalaya, Mt Shivling 1996

Thalay Sagar and the lake Kedar Tal

Himalaya Peak Jogin 1, summit climb

Crestone Needle, Colorado

Athens Marathon, Peter and Andy

Sacramento Bee, Glacier Point Rockfall, June 1999

White Buffalo scar

Glacier Point Apron and Mr. Natural

Pete's Memorial Stone

University Center WSCU Gunnison Colorado

Summit of Mt. Kinabalu Borneo

Black Canyon of the Gunnison

Terbush Tower, photo and route

Aconcagua summit cross with urn of Pete's ashes

PART THREE

COMFORT MY PEOPLE

Chapter 9
Time and Risk

In the mountaineering literature there are instances of climbers when they are at the limit of their personal strength or courage receiving supernatural help. In Shackleton's case it was the extra climber as they crossed over South Georgia Island. Herman Buhl in his epic Nanga Parbat Pilgrimage also recounts a similar instance. Soldiers, sailors, firemen and others have all recorded that at the extreme they were given assistance when they needed it most. I believe this happens much more frequently than people admit. More is going on here than meets the eye. Since the heavenly does interact with our physical world from time to time, I believe that God uses these circumstances and events to build our faith. One of the things most cherished in my life was the promise I heard that night when Peter was so sick, **"I have a plan and a purpose for Peter that you do not understand right now"**. I misunderstood the voice when I thought that building the clinic in Castle Rock was the fulfillment of that promise. I know now that God's plan and purpose for Peter was bigger than that. Peter could have been taken away from us so many times before and in so many places. Particularly during his first three months when he was literally in critical condition, no one really expected that he would live, but he did and thrived. My wife Leigh too was also given help in the form of a dream. When Pete was still in the NICU she dreamed that she saw a boy with curly red hair kicking a soccer ball. She told me about that dream then as it was reassuring to her that Pete would survive. Several years later she remembers exactly that same scene played out on our front lawn, seeing Peter kick that same ball. One of the reasons that God gave us these experiences I believe is to help us and to help others. In second Corinthians it says; "Praise be to the God and father of our Lord Jesus Christ, who comforts us in all our troubles so that we can comfort those in any trouble with the same comfort we ourselves have received".

Not only do these events help us but remind us that God is active and alive and present in the world today. In a recent book by James Carlow and Keith Wall called <u>Encountering Heaven and the Afterlife</u>, the authors describe numerous real-life episodes of people being "touched by an Angel". In one account two young men were climbing when one came off the rock and fell all the way to the ground despite good technique. He landed on his back approximately 50 feet below his climbing partner. When the partner arrived the injured climber "Bobby", described beautiful green fields flowers intense light and music. He also described seeing his grandparents and uncle who had already passed. These stories remind us not only of how transient our lives are but that occasionally, very occasionally, we catch a glimpse of what it is like on the other side. Jim Davidson's recent book called *The Ledge* recounts an instance where at the limits of his ability to climb up 80 feet of over-hanging ice, from the depths of a crevasse on Mount Rainier, his recently departed climbing partner gives him advice and encouragement. So many of these accounts have been written about that there is an entire genre' of books describing these encounters. The poem *Prospice* by Robert Browning describes a near-death experience, (or NDE) and was a favorite poem of Sir Ernest Shackleton;

Prospice by Robert Browning
Fear death?—to feel the fog in my throat,
The mist in my face,
When the snows begin, and the blasts denote
I am nearing the place,
The power of the night, the press of the storm,
The post of the foe;
Where he stands, the Arch Fear in a visible form;
Yet the strong man must go:
For the journey is done and the summit attained,
And the barriers fall,
Though a battle's to fight ere
the guerdon be gained,
The reward of it all.
I was ever a fighter, so—one fight more,
The best and the last!
I would hate that Death bandaged
my eyes, and forbore,
And made me creep past.
No! let me taste the whole of it, fare like my peers,
The heroes of old,
Bear the brunt, in a minute pay glad life's arrears
Of pain, darkness and cold.
For sudden the worst turns the best to the brave.
The black minute's at end,
And the elements' rage, the fiend voices that rave,
Shall dwindle, shall blend,
Shall change, shall become first a peace out of pain.

Then a light, then thy breast,
O thou soul of my soul! I shall clasp thee again,
And with God be the rest!

When God shows his tender mercies and allows us to receive supernatural help it is a supreme gift. The New Testament talks about a "cloud of witnesses" whose example cheers us on. Who are these people who have achieved their high calling; relatives and friends, heroes from ages past, perhaps they are all around us?

Chapter 10
Plans and Planning

Only a few times have I been absolutely certain about a choice. One choice was the decision to ask Leigh to marry me, a good one. Another choice we made was when to start a family. Once we had children there were many more choices; about how to raise them, what to feed them, how to discipline them, how much freedom could they have? And there was plenty of guidance from others. Since we were so young when we got married, in many ways we just grew up alongside our children. We were not the very best parents but we both had good parents. We both learned at home how children were to be nurtured, loved and encouraged to achieve. "Feed 'em and love 'em", was the short version. When we first had our own children, we did not realize the awesome responsibility entrusted to us with those little lives, the result of the decisions we would make were in the future. How families make decisions depends a great deal on what the parents learned when they were growing up. We tended to involve our children, when they were a little older, in most of the big family decisions. Whenever we had the choice to go overseas or do something adventurous we took it. It seemed as a result our children were more open to new ideas, to languages, to culture, to new foods, religion and to meet new people. But you can never know the end from the beginning.

After almost 30 years in the military I feel like I know something about the planning process. General Eisenhower said "plans are nothing but planning is everything". Leigh and I made plans together but were always flexible enough to allow for changes. When opportunities presented themselves we were willing to adapt to take advantage of positive circumstances and hopefully avoid negative ones. "You cannot control the wind but you can adjust your sails", was a quote that Leigh had made into needlepoint and framed, and we keep it on the boat. Good plans need to be based on sufficient knowledge. However you can never know enough about the facts and various possible outcomes of your choices.

I've been fortunate enough to have a dad, Hubert Wayne Terbush, who took a close and personal interest in my plans. His wise counsel saved me from trouble many times. He was an aerospace executive and managed multi-million dollar projects but projected a humble "country" wisdom from his upbringing in Oklahoma. He lived through the Dust Bowl and survived World War II. He would say things like "Jim, remember who you are" and "nothing good ever happens after mid-night". He also stressed the importance of strong family ties and the long term value of advanced education. When I am feeling stressed I will occasionally write him a letter, just to get it off my chest. Sharing at this level is private and special. Fathers and sons rarely get closer than this. I am thankful to have had such a good example in my father.

Likewise, I've had such a good example in my mother, Martha Christina Terbush. She too survived the dustbowl and difficulties growing up in a large, "German/ American" family in Northwest Oklahoma. Her mother was a prayer warrior and she is one too. I knew that whenever I was in trouble (or about to be) she was praying for her son, and for his safe return. Mom changed our family for the better and by her example of faith we too learned to seek guidance from above, Proverbs 19:21.

Chapter 11
Peace Over Time

"The light that burns twice as bright, burns for half as long, and you have burned so very, very brightly,"
Bladerunner, the Movie (1982)

We never know what effect our lives are having on others. When we went back for Peter's Memorial in Castle Rock many people came up to me to remember specific instances of either how I had been responsible for their healthcare or stories about Peter. We constantly leave a legacy, like it or not, as we move forward. There are several nice stories from Peter's friends sent to us shortly after he died. One was from Alex Eaton who wrote "I remember Peter teaching me how to ice climb and how hard he laughed at my terrified face looking down into the roaring abyss of the Ouray (Colorado) Ice Park. If I hadn't already known his skills as a climber and instructor I would've been much more concerned by his nonchalant instructions. 'Climb back up, and don't chop your rope!' Later the same day as the light was dimming and I was left to pull the ice screws on the hardest climb I've ever tried, I got jammed up and nervous. Despite my somewhat precarious situation I laughed in spite of myself listening to the whistled tune of Bob Marley's "Small Axe" as Peter down climbed without a rope to give a little moral support. I felt better just watching how fluid he was, a huge smile across his dirty face, his white beat-up helmet always seeming to be a little cockeyed on his head.... Peter never wasted a moment in life; he seized every second as an opportunity to live life to the fullest".

Another friend of his, Kari Nierling, wrote a short poem, reprinted below;

"With curly hair and a bounce in his
walk it made us laugh to hear him talk.
He tell a story that was much too long or whistled
loudly a random song.
He was always disappearing at least once a day with
a smile and his laugh, "no worries" he'd say. Remember
the time he slept in the tree and how
we roamed happy and carefree.
He showed no anger, nor a trace of meanness....
and we all know he wasn't the cleanest!
So full of life, dreams and love, when
the warm sun shines its Peter above.
He never let go even at the end.
Peter Terbush is the meaning of friend."

The Scripture John 15:13 "Greater love has no one than this, that a man lay down his life for his friends", has been closely associated with Pete and his actions in Yosemite. On a Christian website called Lifeline they wrote, "Peter didn't run. With amazing courage he grasped the rope with all his strength and accepted his own loss of life so that his friend might live. Later, when his lifeless broken body was dug out from the massive pile of rocks, this discovery was made: Peter's hands, which had kept the rope steady for Kerry, were still clenching his friends lifeline! This courageous act is a glimmer of what Christ did for you and me. He faced a cruel death on the cross, though he was sinless, so that we could experience new life and the forgiveness of our sins. It was the greatest act of love and compassion the world has ever known. And it came with intense suffering and death. Much like a friend holding onto a lifeline for another, we can help and strengthen others as they see us boldly live our faith. And we can be of tremendous support to them. Do what's right even if it leads to suffering. Don't let go of the Lifeline". The Solid Rock Climbers for Christ, www.srcfc.org / Peter Terbush Story, talks about how Pete's story has been used as an example of Christ's love for all of us. "Pete's death and self-sacrifice shows the sacred responsibility we have when we hold the ropes for our climbing partners. More importantly, his courageous act reminds us clearly of how Jesus Christ held the rope to save us. These words are found in the Bible, 'You see, at just the right time, when we were still powerless, Christ died for the ungodly. Very rarely will anyone die for a righteous man, though for a good man someone might possibly dare to die. But God demonstrates his own love for us in this: While we were still sinners, Christ died for us'", Romans 5:6-8.

His younger cousin James Throckmorton wrote "Peter's story inspired me to encourage me and my friends to be the best that we can be, make the best use of our time, and show love to one another. To do this I started an electronic newsletter highlighting the growth of Heroes through their youth, and illustrating how they used their time for the good of others. As Peter was invested in my life, it pays dividends in the lives of others".

Justin Lean who climbed Peak Jogin 1 with us in India wrote, "I consider Pete my best climbing partner. Peter never ever hurt a soul and often his enthusiasm would encourage me to overcome my own fears and climb with more gusto. Though my association with the Singapore Everest expedition has given me the opportunity to climb in different parts of the world, the trip I treasure most is not Everest but the one to Jogin 1 in the Gharwal

Himalaya with Pete and Jim. The climbing was among friends, completely free of national obligations, unlike Everest."

Pete's sometime employer and director of Wilderness Pursuits (WP), at Western State Colorado University, Matt Tyler, wrote "Peter thrived, clinging to the face of a cliff or a pinnacle of ice. To him breathing thin mountain air was like breathing pure rich life. His eyes seemed to glow as he discussed his next goal or challenge. Peter climbed with the grace and easy movement of the cat". Continuing Matt said, "Peter, as part of a WP staff group, was taking part in training just two weeks before his death. After climbing the Crestone Needle, 14,203', Pete said: 'you know guys, this climb we just did was a lot easier than the last time I was here, but I liked it a lot better.' When asked why Pete replied again 'I came here not for the risk or the adrenaline, but because it's the greatest way to get to know great people.' Peter would climb with anyone. He came to WP and gave of his time in order to help others". http://www.summitpost.org/crestone-needle/150434

Sean Matusewicz wrote about a first ascent of an 800' spire in the Black Canyon of the Gunnison; "we named it the 'Terbush Tower' and the route 'Good Skills'", a compliment which Peter would give to another climber. Sean describes the climbing route itself in detail for others to follow, but also wrote a short narrative that was meaningful to me. "The idea of putting up the new route didn't dawn on us until the moment was right and tangibly sitting in front of us. We had rappelled into the Black Canyon of the Gunnison River planning to do 'Maidens Voyage', a short albeit classic route best described as "an intro to the Black". When we got there another party was on it and instead of waiting or looking for another trade route our eyes fixed on a beautiful 800 foot tower. Splitter cracks ran its length, while the whole buttress sat slightly detached from the canyon rim, its western edge just catching the warm Colorado rays." He goes on to describe how their instructor, Courtney Scales, a veteran of the "Black" described how he couldn't quite explain all the things that factored into the decision to guide his students on virgin territory. All the safety aspects were there, they were competent climbers, the route had been thoroughly scoped, even looked at for years, but other things he said, "deep things" entered into it as well. "For me it felt like the group was no longer in control, almost as if a silent partner had prepared everything, urging us to ascend the new route". Sean then goes on to describe the climb itself in detail, then finishes with a few comments about reaching the summit. "A quick inspection revealed no "rap" slings or gear and confirmed our hopes of the virgin status. We each sat silently for a moment contemplating what it means to stand where no man has stood before. With the sun still high in the sky we rapped off the tower into a narrow cliffed out gully and racked up for one last exit pitch. As we reached the canyon's rim and the true end of the climb, a golden eagle, wings spread wide, soared overhead and let out a tremendous screech. He circled for a long time watching just a few meters above. It was a tangible moment much like the beginning of the climb that reminded us that "sending" is sometimes more than just rock-climbing.

These wonderful stories have many similarities and they give me hope. One of my favorites is from a friend of Pete's named Laura Chase. She describes how she met Peter in the first few weeks of her freshman year at college and remembers the exact moment, especially his crazy laugh, his energy and his wild curly hair. Laura was already an accomplished rock climber but Pete showed her how to aid climb on a big wall route in Zion National Park. She describes one of the last pitches which traversed slightly and she was having trouble cleaning the pitch. She kept swinging away from the route. "Then Peter called down from above", she says. He asked "how are you doing?" and I yelled back that

I couldn't get the gear we had placed for protection. With utmost sincerity and without hesitation he continued to shout encouragement and told me to, "just leave it and continue". This happened again and again, "you've got to be kidding me", I thought. After more flailed attempts he yelled down again, "its okay Laura just leave it, that was a bad placement, my fault". Again Peter would say "bad placement, no worries, my bad, you're doing great" and by the time I had reached the top I'd left a good amount of booty for the next lucky party to climb the route. Pete never mentioned a word about the gear instead he congratulated me on getting to the top of my first big wall. That last pitch could have made the difference between loving the climb and hating the climb and it might have turned me off to aid climbing forever, but because of the way Pete handled the situation that wall remains one of my best memories, and the smile on my face when I got to the belay was all the thanks he needed".

Kerry Pyle, who was with Peter that fateful day in Yosemite also wrote from his heart a beautiful narrative about their friendship. Just a short excerpt gives you a sense of the mystical quality of two climbers sharing a rope. "Methodically, with movements ingrained like a sixth sense, you swing pitch after pitch. Your very life is entrusted to his diligent watch below. Understanding and comfort send reassuring encouragement up through the umbilical cord that attaches you together. Anger, fear, doubt, joy, anxiety and love are all portrayed in your movements. This you tell yourself is the ultimate goal in life, to achieve companionship as great as this."

So many people wrote kind words about to Pete that we continue to be comforted even so many years later. One of the reasons I love to go to the Summit in Gunnison each year is to hear new stories about Peter from his friends. These things reassure me that Peter was indeed true to his values, true to his friends and to his faith.

Chapter 12
Reunion

Should old acquaintance be forgot,
and never brought to mind ?
Should old acquaintance be forgot, and old lang syne ?
Robert Burns 1788

Will we ever see our loved ones again? Do they have any interaction with us while we are here on earth? Do they have good and useful work to accomplish in Heaven? A number of books have been written on the subject; <u>Heaven</u> by Randy Alcorn says "yes" to all of the above and backs it up with scripture verses. Another book, <u>Heaven, Your True Home</u>, written by Joni Eareckson Tada, has a remarkable tone of hope for someone who has been confined to a wheelchair since she was 17 years old. She too describes Heaven as a place of unspeakable joy and boundless opportunities. They would both agree that the (good) skills and traits we have gained from living on the earth continue with us. A favorite scripture in the book of Hebrews, Chapter 12;1, goes like this "since we are surrounded by such a great cloud of witnesses, let us throw off everything that hinders and the sin that so easily entangles, and let us run with perseverance the race marked out for us". So many of the stories in the Bible that relate to life after death seem to indicate that the departed continue to at least observe and possibly intervene on our behalf. Other books about heaven and end-of-life experiences are so eerily similar that one must give credence to these accounts. That we are able to see our loved ones again, without disease or injury, and to be fully present with our Savior is almost too much to be hoped for.

I can imagine that Peter is still helping others, especially rock climbers and mountaineers in distress. How often do climbers find themselves in a situation where they send up a quick prayer and then things just "work out?" It is hopeful to me to think that persons who are cold and alone and frightened sometimes get supernatural help. I myself have found that shooting up just a quick "bullet" prayer often changes my circumstances and gives me peace. The idea that there is only a very thin partition between this life and the next is reassuring, humbling and awesome. The idea of being constantly back-and-forth in prayer is not a new one. It was recommended in the New Testament by Paul and has been practiced by persons of faith ever since. I think that the ideal circumstance might be where I am in continuous contact with the Creator and able to carry out his purposes without restraint of time and space. That is what I imagine Heaven to be like and that is what I hope Peter is doing right now.

Members of the Armed Forces of the United States; Army, Air Force, Navy, Marine Corps and Coast Guard, are in harm's way right now. Family members back home wait and pray every day for a safe return. I was a physician in the US Navy for almost 30 years and appreciate what courage and bravery our Nation's warriors display in battle. I was given a prayer card to keep in my wallet by a Catholic Chaplain, and have treasured it since.

The Saint Michael Prayer

Saint Michael the Archangel,
defend us in the day of battle.
Be our safeguard against the wickedness and the
snares of the devil.
May God rebuke him we humbly pray and do thou
O Prince of the Heavenly Host,
cast into hell Satan and all the evil spirits who
prowl throughout the world
seeking the ruin of souls.
Amen

We pray before battle, we pray for strength and courage, we pray for the defeat our enemies and we pray for the fallen. I believe our soldiers are also given supernatural help in battle, when they escape death or injury but also when they fall. Numerous families across the United States, are grieving for loved ones right now. Young people who had bright futures ahead of them are gone. But I believe they are still alive in Heaven and aware of what is happening on earth below, and this gives me comfort. How we as individuals deal with grief and loss is very personal. Difficult circumstances of a loved one's death will certainly color the process. Each person has their own "holocaust" type experience. We were so very fortunate that Peter, as far as we know, did not suffer.

He was also doing the thing he loved and living life to the fullest there in Yosemite. That in the process of saving another person's life he lost his own seems congruent for someone who lived life so intensely and so well. I do believe that Pete is in the "bleachers" with the rest of the crowd cheering us on. We all certainly hope to finish well and while we are on this planet, for just a short space of time, to accomplish the things that God meant for us to do. Although I could not see the end from the beginning of Pete's life, I can see now that Pete's early birth, life and sacrificial death were all part of God's plan, "a plan and a purpose", I did not understand then. I see things coming full circle with meaning, trust and love for a Creator who is able to work all things together for good. Romans 8:28.

Afterword

This book ended up being a gift for me as I remembered all the good (and some of the bad) that happened in the life of our son. Writing this book has caused emotional highs and lows, but I believe my grieving is over, I am resolved now, I can take the next steps without anguish, or worry about where Pete is or what he is doing. I have faith that God, who has Peter in his hands, will protect and comfort him where there are no tears, sickness or injury. My bride still struggles with this concept and will continue to work through her grief in a different way. I am reminded that life is precious and sweet. It is frequently beautiful. We know for sure it is short. For the fortunate few who enjoy a full life, without debilitating loss or illness, it could possibly be taken for granted. For the rest of us who have suffered loss, our challenge is to find the good which remains and squeeze all the life and meaning "into" our experiences. If we choose to make that our decision, then we are the fortunate ones. No one knows how much time he or she still has. When my time is through, and I am welcomed home, I hope to be able to stand there with Peter, look at some far away peak and say, "let's go for it!"

Date: November 21, 2008 National Park Service News bulletin

On October 7 and 8, 2008, two rockfalls occurred in Yosemite Valley, affecting the Curry Village area. This resulted in the temporary closure of many of the visitor accommodations until a thorough geologic assessment could be completed. During this time, National Park Service (NPS) geologists, in collaboration with the U.S. Geological Survey, and other national and international scientists, conducted extensive investigation and study of rockfalls that have occurred in the area above Curry Village using the latest scientific mapping and computer modeling techniques. The analysis has shown that approximately 6,000 cubic meters of rock were involved in the events.

With the increased overall frequency of rockfall over the past few years, in conjunction with the geologic research that has been conducted, the NPS can no longer treat each rockfall as an isolated incident. Instead, we must look at the area comprehensively and recognize that geologic processes that have shaped Yosemite Valley since the last glaciers receded will continue to result in rockfall.

Based on the above information, the NPS has decided to close 233 visitor accommodations (tent cabins, cabins with bath, cabins without bath) permanently. This will also permanently close associated visitor support structures (shower house, restrooms, etc.) and 43 concessioner employee housing units. This accounts for approximately one third of the units in Curry Village available to park visitors.

Additionally, 36 visitor accommodations (tent cabins and cabins with bath) that were temporarily closed will reopen to the public today. While the NPS cannot say that the occupancy of these units, and the units never closed, are totally risk free, we firmly believe that the risk remaining at Curry Village is roughly the same level of risk that exists in other areas of Yosemite Valley in which structures are located such as The Ahwahnee and Yosemite Village. Rockfalls are natural occurrences that have shaped, and continue to shape Yosemite Valley. The natural processes that contribute to rockfall are part of the dynamics of nature. Though impossible to predict or control, ongoing scientific analysis is being conducted to further understand this phenomenon.

About the author

Jim Terbush is a "Salty ol' Sailor" with almost 30 years of Service in the US Navy. He and his bride "Leigh" have lived in six different countries and visited more than 80. In 2000 he and Leigh sailed from Capetown South Africa to Buenos Aires, Argentina in their 40 ft. sailboat, the Blue Peter. Jim has a love of wild places and has worked in both the Arctic and Antarctica, serving as Ship's Doctor. He is a member of the James Caird Society (Shackleton) and has spoken to many groups about Resilience and Servant Leadership principles. Jim Terbush and his wife Leigh live in Manitou Springs Colorado where they enjoy the mountains and look forward to growing old and wrinkled, together.

Through the Valley of the Shadow is Jim's first book.

If you would like to help participate in training Servant Leaders and Mountain Guides in the Rocky Mountains, you may make a tax-deductible (in the US) gift contribution to; WSCU Foundation, 600 North Adams Street, Gunnison, CO 81231, Tel; 970.943.7051.